JOSH WOOD

STRUGGLE BUS

THE VAN. THE MYTH. THE LEGEND.

Smile! You own the most ridiculous book of 2020.

LUCIDBOOKS

Struggle Bus
The Van. The Myth. The Legend

Copyright © 2020 by Josh Wood

Published by Lucid Books in Houston, TX
www.LucidBooksPublishing.com

ISBN-10: 1-63296-392-2
ISBN-13: 978-1-63296-392-5
eISBN-10: 1-63296-429-5
eISBN-13: 978-1-63296-429-8

Unless otherwise indicated, Scripture quotations are taken from the ESV® Bible (The Holy Bible, English Standard Version®), copyright © 2001 by Crossway, a publishing ministry of Good News Publishers. Used by permission. All rights reserved.

Scripture quotations marked (KJV) are taken from the King James Version (KJV): King James Version, public domain.

Special Sales: Most Lucid Books titles are available in special quantity discounts. Custom imprinting or excerpting can also be done to fit special needs. Contact Lucid Books at Info@ LucidBooksPublishing.com.

Table of Contents

Introduction

During the summer of 2018, the time came to part ways with our 2005 Ford van. I dreaded the whole van-selling process for a myriad of reasons. Cleaning. Describing. Posting. Haggling. To quote the venerable 2012 Internet sensation Kimberly "Sweet Brown" Wilkins, "Ain't nobody got time for that." Also, big-family van years work like dog years; one year of wear and tear in our world equals seven years of wear and tear in the world of normal human vehicle usage. Our van was basically 91 years old. It wasn't hard to predict how the dreaded sales process would go. It would go like this.

I post an ad on Craigslist. A potential buyer reads the ad and expresses interest in the van. The two of us take valuable time out of our respective schedules and arrange a time to meet. At this meeting, some variation of the following conversation occurs.

> Potential buyer: "So, how's the air-conditioning?"
> Me: "Well, about that. . ."
> Potential buyer: "So, how's the sound system?"
> Me: "Well, about that. . ."
> Potential buyer: "What else is wrong with it?"
> Me: "You're going to want to have a seat. This is going to take a while."

Ain't nobody got time for that. I only had time in my schedule for exactly one of those conversations. In an effort to save time for everyone involved, I decided I would opt for full disclosure when creating the ad. Sure, it would take a little more time initially, but it would save me an enormous amount of time in the long run. So I got to work. My wife, Careese, and I sat down, and I started typing. We laughed and laughed as we discussed the van's many issues and the stories of how they came to be. "No one is ever going to buy this thing," we agreed. Oh well. We'll post the ad anyway. If no one is interested in a couple weeks, we'll lower the price and try again. I uploaded a few unprofessional photos and clicked "post."

What followed was unbelievable. We never imagined that our pathetic old van would soon give the Internet a good laugh. Within 24 hours of posting the Craigslist ad, messages were pouring in from across the country. Families were sharing eerily similar stories. People we'd never met were thanking us for the laughs. Many were even suggesting fixes for the van's many problems. The whole thing was such a blessing to us. So fun. We loved reading the stories. It restored my hope in society's use of the Internet.

Among the messages was a surprising number of "You should write more" messages. After a couple weeks, I finally convinced myself to write a book based on the now-viral Craigslist post.

Will Rogers said, "If Stupidity got us into this mess, then why can't it get us out?"[1]

While I was fully aware of how ridiculous "write a book based on a Craigslist post" sounds in the literary world, I talked myself into a bad idea with this rationalization: if people enjoyed commiserating with me so much about one little Craigslist post, perhaps they'll enjoy commiserating with our family through more stories about our van, our family, and our life.

This book, *The Struggle Bus*, was thus born. And don't worry. The one-of-a-kind literary adventure on which you are about to embark is not so much about the van itself as it is about life with a big family. It's about parenting. It's about marriage. It's about success. It's about failure. It's about the Struggle Bus becoming a metaphor for our lives as we gave it a fun-filled beatdown for the ages. Before I get to those stories, however, a little background is in order.

Our family is not normal. At all. There was a time, however, when it was closer to normal. We had 2.3 kids. We drove a normal-sized vehicle. We washed and dried a normal amount of laundry. We ate dinner sitting down. We slept sometimes. Our house was clean. We didn't spend our time

---

1. "Will Rogers Quotes," *Goodreads*, https://www.goodreads.com/quotes/7253122-if -stupidity-got-us-into-this-mess-then-why-can-t.

searching for missing shoes. Or coats. Or toothbrushes. Or the source of horrendous odors. Or sanity.

Then came the crazy.

In the span of 20 months, our family of four grew to a family of eight. Our six kids were ages five, three, two, one, one, and a newborn. For those of you keeping score at home, yes, we had four kids in diapers; and yes, we had six kids in car seats. Any sense of normalcy vanished. Our couch would never again function as a comfortable place for sitting. It would henceforth serve as the sturdy foundation of a perpetual laundry mountain. That didn't really matter, though, because we rarely sat down anymore and, thus, had no use for comfortable places to sit, relax, or sleep. I'm pretty sure that we slept for a combined two hours in two years. Despite our best attempts, our house became, well, not clean. There was no time for that because we spent 50 percent of our day changing diapers, 50 percent of our day preparing meals, 50 percent of our day cleaning up the unholy mess of carnage that was created at meal time, 50 percent of our day bathing children, and the rest of our time searching for missing shoes, coats, toothbrushes, and more. Seriously, though, WHERE DO MY KIDS KEEP PUTTING THEIR SHOES?

You get the point. Mid-2007 through 2009 was a blur of total chaos. It was adorable chaos, but chaos nonetheless. God bless our family and friends who put up with us during that time. We lived in survival mode for a couple of years. Like any family, we had highs, and we had lows, but we loved it. We had a blast. We cherished it. We prayed a lot. We'd do it again in a heartbeat. We learned an abundance of life lessons. You know the saying "God won't give you more than you can handle"? Yeah, that's a stupid saying. What's that? You would like me to back up that statement biblically? Sure, I will. Thanks for asking. Here's one of many examples: Gideon. God intentionally picked the weakest member of the weakest tribe to lead a tiny group of soldiers—a group so small that it was completely incapable of handling the task given to it. Why did God choose Gideon and his merry band of water-lapping, would-be losers? He did it to leave no doubt as to *who* earned the victory. Story of our life.

Eventually, we settled into our new normal. We began to breathe. That proverbial breath lasted about a day. Then our family got even bigger. I blame my oldest daughter. You see, for at least two years (every night without fail) she had been praying for God to give her a big sister. At first, I would give her a patronizing little pat on the head and try to prepare her for inevitable disappointment. I tried to explain that giving birth to an older sibling was physically impossible. I tried to explain that God doesn't always answer prayers with a yes. She was undeterred.

"...and please, God, give me a big sister. Amen." Every. Night.

After a while, I gave up trying to reason with her. "Just talk to Jesus about it" became a common refrain. Then the craziest thing happened. Following a series of wild and unexpected events, a teenager moved into our house. The plan was for her to stay for a week or two. A week or two turned into permanent. Our household increased to nine. We entered a foreign world of curfews and dating and cliques and teenage driving. People warned us that teenagers were awful. As it turns out, teenagers can be wonderful. Teenagers can be amazing big sisters. In fact, our daughter stopped praying for a big sister. Her prayers changed. "Thank you, God, for giving me a big sister." It's humbling to hear the words "I told you so" from a seven-year-old, especially 2,801 times. In fact, she still tells us "I told you so" all these years later. It's our constant, beautiful reminder that we aren't in control and that our plans can't compare to God's plans.

Side note: This is what the Bible is talking about when it talks about childlike faith. Adults tend to put God in a box as if there are things that are off-limits in the world of prayer. Kids don't think like that. Happily, I've never heard the end of it.

That brings me to the now-famous van. You see, math defeated us: 2 adults + 1 teenager + 6 kids in car seats = our old SUV was no longer of adequate size. Ultimately, in 2009, we decided that a 12-passenger van would probably be the best option for our family since we often found ourselves toting around kids' friends in addition to our own kids. Off to Craigslist I went in search of a 12-passenger van. My wife and I reminded each other of our newlywed days. Back then, we said we would never become those nerdy parents who drove a minivan. We were too cool for that. . .or something. We made a number of other statements that turned out to be reverse-prophetic:

"We'll never move back to our hometown!"
"We'll never be those parents who bribe our kids with candy in Walmart!"
"We'll never homeschool our kids!"
"Our kids will never throw a fit in public like that!"
. . .and perhaps the most famous of all our "nevers". . .
"I'll never be pregnant again." (Careese)

I'm convinced there's some angel out there whose sole task is to gallivant around the world listening for the words "I'll never" or "we'll never." As soon as said angel hears some fool utter those immortal words, he leaps into action, focusing all his supernatural energy on turning the negative statement into a positive reality.

You see, our prayerful little daughter started praying for another baby. It seems to be our pattern that just about the time our other kids are out of diapers and we feel as though we can stop and take a breath, another baby, followed by another 22 months later, arrives. Our latest additions to the family were born ready to throw fuel on the fire that would one day become the resale value of the Struggle Bus.

Oh, to be young and stupid. My wife and I both laughed (and maybe cried a little) as we realized we were skipping right over nerdy minivans and leaping into the land of church vans and buses. Suddenly, minivans didn't seem so bad. Suddenly, minivans seemed super desirable. At the time, one of our friends had just purchased a new Toyota Sienna. He let us drive it. Those things are sweet! I was jealous. Over a minivan! Alas, there would be no sweet-riding minivans for our family. A mega-van it would be. Let's summarize. Pre-children Josh and Careese: "Minivans are for parents who've traded dignity for functionality." Parental Josh and Careese: "We like big bus, and we cannot lie."

That's where this story begins—with the purchase of the van that our teenager would later name "the Struggle Bus." The stories you are about to read revolve around the struggle-bus-ness of our van and our lives. My wife and I hope our ridiculous stories give you as much laughter as they've given us. Be blessed.

Oh, and if you have never seen the ad that made the Struggle Bus famous, please take a minute to check it out below. It will help you make sense of the rest of this book. Here you go:

We're selling our 2005 Ford E350 XL Extended 15 passenger van. Photos attached. In the interest of full disclosure, here's more information and a partial list of its issues. Please read before making an offer. Thanks!

The van is missing a speaker in the side door. My kids have been throwing random items in the speaker hole for years. So, you may end up with some very special treasures. Or really old chicken nuggets. Probably both.

One side of the van has a yellow scuff mark on it. That's courtesy of me and a battle with a yellow concrete parking divider (I did not win). The other side of the van has a matching white scuff mark. That one is courtesy of my wife. She completes me. In related news, you know how most cars these days come equipped with a fancy backup camera? This one does not.

My wife and I have used this van for the better part of a decade. We're a lovely couple, but we sometimes inadvertently back into inanimate objects. Also, we've been forced to take defensive driving classes a few more times than the average American. That said, there are a number of other minor scratches, dents, and places where the paint is chipped on this vehicle.

When you open the side doors, the rubber door liner is detached in some places. It still does its job, but it looks stupid.

The van came equipped with automatic door locks. Unfortunately, they no longer work. Somehow, something got reversed, and the locking motor ran without ceasing until the button was pressed and held down. Rather than taking the van to a repair shop like a normal person, I duct taped the button down to keep the motor from running. At some point, the duct tape failed, and the motor ran until it eventually burned up or something. Anyhow, the automatic door locks don't work. Each door must be locked and unlocked manually. Duct tape is not included.

We're a family of 11. Every one of our children has thrown up in this van at some point in the past decade—most notably on this trip: http://www.josh woodtx.com/college-station-2015/. We have had the van detailed a couple times since then (shout out to Xtreme Auto Re-Styling Center for tackling a level of depravity unrivaled in the world of passenger transport.) The van is clean now, but it will probably always be inhabited by the ghost of vomit past.

The automatic windows work! This is good because the air conditioner does not. Well, it sort of works and sort of doesn't. It works fine until you accelerate past 45 miles per hour. After that, the gas pedal essentially functions as an on/off switch for the air conditioner. Accelerate = AC off. Decelerate = AC on. I don't understand why. But, then again, as you've probably gathered by now, I don't understand most things about cars.

The windshield is cracked.

There's a 20″ TV mounted to the ceiling. It works and is connected to an in-dash DVD player. This is a handy feature as it helps distract kids from the intermittent air conditioning and smell of decaying chicken nuggets.

I don't think that the front speakers work. Actually, just assume that they don't. Better yet, if you're wondering if some particular part of the van works, just assume it doesn't work in the way that Ford originally intended it to work.

I looked the van up on Kelley Blue Book. $4,396. Unfortunately, Kelley Blue Book only allows me to choose between the following conditions: excellent, very good, good, and fair. I chose "fair" since "sad" was not an option. I've adjusted my asking price accordingly.

The heater works. Also, the van has a hitch and wiring for a trailer.

In order to save myself a bit of time answering requests for more information, I've decided to add a FAQ section below:

FAQ

Q: "Have you performed all proper maintenance and religiously changed the oil every 3,000 miles?"

A: [laughter] No. No, I have not. Does this article make you feel better? It made me feel better. https://www.nytimes.com/2010/09/11/your-money/11short cuts.html.

Q: "Are those 143,000 miles mostly highway miles?"

A: Well, a lot of them are. However, we've been using this van as our farm van for the past year or so. Also, in efforts to find quicker routes, I've been known to disobey Siri's directions. These "shortcuts" have sometimes taken us on exotic, off-road adventures. I'm pretty sure those miles cancel out all of the so-called "highway miles."

Q: "Is the registration current?"

A: Yes! It should be noted, however, that the first three letters of the current license plate are FRT. We have five boys under the age of 12 in our house. This is a very unfortunate combination.

Q: "How are the tires and the brakes?"

A: They seem to be ok; but, as with everything else, I recommend getting them checked out. I did buy the tires at Discount Tire, so there's a warranty with them.

One last note: I recommend getting this thing checked over by a mechanic before buying. Everything under the hood looks and sounds fine to me; but, then again, I would have no idea if it didn't look or sound right.

CHAPTER 1
HEY, HONEY, DON'T HATE ME,
I SORTA DID A THING

It was 2009, and the Wood family was all set to take a begrudging leap into the market of 12-passenger vans. There was virtually no chance this leap was going to end well. How could it? I knew little about cars and less about vans. Fortunately, in his infinite wisdom, a generous God brought the likes of Sergey Brin and Larry Page into the world to create Google. And Google gives car idiots like me a chance at success. I grabbed my laptop, spent far too much time creating a wonderful little spreadsheet, and then commenced with van research. I started by googling all these van things I was too embarrassed to ask other people:

diesel vs. regular vans
What does the V in V8 engine stand for?
Do I have to have a CDL to drive a 12-passenger van?
cost of Mercedes van
cheapest 12-passenger vans
Ford vs. Chevy
Do people buy old limos instead of vans?
Do I have to have a CDL to drive a limo?
Lamborghini limo
Lamborghini
Cost to rent a Lamborghini
Sale price of a kidney (just kidding)

Anyhow, I eventually reentered reality and resumed my search for van-related knowledge. After a couple of hours, I had learned enough to make a slightly informed decision. The decision: our next van would be a four-, five-, or six-year-old, 12-passenger, Ford E350 van. With a bit of searching (and a bit more off-task Lamborghini browsing because the new Gallardo is a thing of beauty), I was able to locate a number of vans that fit my criteria on Craigslist, Cars.com, and eBay. Unfortunately, none of these vans were located in Amarillo, Texas. My closest option was approximately four hours away in Albuquerque, New Mexico. I called up the seller and talked through the details over the phone (in 2009, people still used their phones for old-school voice-to-voice communication). I asked all the questions Google told me I should ask when buying a van. After the seller answered every question to my satisfaction, I was excited to make a deal (well, as excited as one can be when shopping for used 12-passenger vans). We agreed on a price, and I—along with my dad, who, God bless him, agreed to drive me four hours to meet a stranger for a Craigslist deal—headed to Albuquerque to pay the man.

When I arrived, the owner gave me the keys, and I gave the exterior a good once-over. Everything looked as it should. Next, I popped open the hood and examined everything. Full disclosure: by "examined everything," I mean "pretended I had the slightest clue what I was looking at." What was under the hood looked exactly like an engine, so I figured I was good to go. Then I hopped into the driver's seat and looked around the inside of the van. The inside seemed a bit large, even for a 12-passenger van, so I counted seats and seatbelts. Fifteen. Fifteen? I had just driven more than four hours to Albuquerque to buy a giant 12-passenger van only to find out the van I had tentatively committed to was, in fact, an even giant-er 15-passenger van. Ugh! So I did what many great men have done throughout history: I rationalized. I rationalized until my mistake, in my mind, had morphed from an embarrassing failure into a wonderful stroke of good luck. I thought to myself, "Since I was getting a good deal on a 12-passenger van, I suppose I am getting an even better deal on a 15-passenger van. It also might be nice to have the extra room for the veritable cornucopia of parenting gear our family takes along with us on road trips. And I've driven all this way, and everything else looks great. Sold!" We signed the papers, and I started my drive home.

About 30 seconds into my drive home, it dawned on me that my sweet wife might not be too thrilled that we now owned an extended 15-passenger van rather than the prediscussed 12-passenger van. What had I done? There is a feeling that all husbands experience at some point in their married lives. It's a unique feeling that comes just a moment after an act of monumental stupidity when he knows he is going to have to explain [insert act of monumental stupidity] to his wife. It's an eerily similar feeling to the feeling all dads get when their child reaches a certain height and said child's running hugs transform little heads and flailing arms into weapons of mass destruction. Anyhow, I got "the feeling." I prayed a little. I pulled over to the side of the road. Then I made the call.

"Hey, honey. Don't hate me. I sorta did a thing. I accidentally bought a 15-passenger van instead of a 12-passenger van. But, you know, I was thinking that it'd be better anyway because [insert all my semi-logical explanations for why I wasn't an idiot]."

"Sounds great to me. We really might enjoy having the extra space. It could actually work out better for us, anyway," she replied (after a healthy dose of sarcasm-laced harassment).

Unsolicited advice for any single guys out there reading this book: marry an optimist. Actually, marry a sarcastic, quick-witted optimist like I did. They're funnier.

I got off the phone and breathed a sigh of relief. She's the best. Back on the road again.

I glanced down at the gas gauge. Dang it! The little orange arrow was pointing directly at the letter *E*. I stopped at the next gas station. I pulled up to the gas pump, unscrewed the gas cap, and panicked. Had I bought a diesel van or a regular van? I had specified "regular" rather than "diesel" in my Craigslist search, but I had also specified "12-passenger" not "15-passenger." I hadn't thought to ask the seller to clarify before I drove off. The gas cap was no help. The owner's manual was no help. I had no idea what would happen if you put regular gas in a diesel engine, but I figured it probably wouldn't be good. I didn't deserve to be a van owner. I spent 20 minutes (not an exaggeration) searching through all the van documentation trying to decide what to do. Should I call the previous owner? Should I call Ford's customer service number? Should I flip a coin and take a chance? Ultimately, I decided there was no option that allowed me to drive away with my dignity. So I called the previous owner. Straight to voicemail. Ugh! After 10 minutes or so on Google, I was 82 percent sure that the van took regular gasoline. I took my chances. I filled the thing all the way up with regular gas, prayed a little, and drove off. When I saw no smoke after 10 miles or so, I figured everything was going to work out just fine.

As you will soon see, everything did not work out just fine, but it worked out fun. It's been quite the ride.

The Struggle Bus, as we came to call it, would become a pretty good metaphor for parenting and life. That I-don't-deserve-to-be-a-van-owner feeling I'd had in the midst of my gasoline conundrum felt all too familiar. Truth be told, from diaper number one, I've had an I-don't-deserve-to-be-a-baby-owner feeling. To be fair, diaper number one is probably the least human thing babies do. I don't want to spoil the surprise for those of you who haven't yet had the luxury of changing a baby's first diaper, but I'm going to. Imagine that your baby's rear end has been dipped into a mixture of tar, rubber cement, and superglue. It's like that. Babies don't come with an owner's manual. We once filled one of our babies up with regular milk for a few weeks before we figured out that we had a lactose-intolerant model. The results were decidedly messier than if I had put diesel in our regular gasoline van. But we prayed, sought wise counsel, adapted, and changed.

Sometimes in parenting, as in Struggle Bus driving, Google isn't any help. If there were such a thing as an owner's manual or a customer service number, it wouldn't always help, either. As you will soon read, whether it's repairing a speaker hole or mending an owie or navigating rural back roads in Oklahoma or helping your kids perform in front of a crowd of Kenyans, sometimes you just make an educated guess and hope to God that everything turns out okay. Then, when things don't turn out okay, you pray, seek wise counsel, adapt, and change.

From day one, our van has lived up to its name. It's a messy, pride-killing, kid-filled, smelly beast of a vehicle—and we've had the time of our lives making it that way. In other words, what started out as an intimidating mess of a van purchase has transformed into our spirit animal: the Struggle Bus.

Thus begins the story of the van, the myth, the legend.

CHAPTER 2
THE SPEAKER HOLE AND AV SYSTEM

Remember our ad when we decided to sell the Struggle Bus in 2018?

> *The van is missing a speaker in the side door. My kids have been throwing random items in the speaker hole for years. So you may end up with some very special treasures. Or really old chicken nuggets. Probably both.*
>
> *There's a 20" TV mounted to the ceiling. It works and is connected to an in-dash DVD player. This is a handy feature as it helps distract kids from the intermittent air conditioning and smell of decaying chicken nuggets.*
>
> *I don't think that the front speakers work. Actually, just assume that they don't. Better yet, if you're wondering if some particular part of the van works, just assume it doesn't work in the way that Ford originally intended it to work.*

The speaker in the side door had been a problem from the beginning. It wasn't too long after I'd driven the van home in 2009 that we noticed an odd lack of sound coming from that speaker. Upon closer inspection, it was obvious that the speaker cover had been haphazardly superglued on. Weird. I pried the cover off and discovered an empty hole where the speaker should have been. Son of a bass thumper.

I was more annoyed with the lack of speaker than your average, speaker-less Joe. You see, music is a big deal in our family. Allow me to explain.

For starters, we have at least one theme song for every road trip. We've listened to all of these:

"Take It Easy" by the Eagles on a corner in Winslow, Arizona.

"King of New York" (and the entire *Newsies* soundtrack on repeat) in New York.

The "Aggie War Hymn" as we drove into College Station, Texas.

A large variety of songs from various Disney movies as we rode into Disney World.

Seventeen kid-appropriate seconds of "California Love" by Tupac as we drove into California.

"Africa" by Toto and "Waka Waka" by Shakira as we drove out of Nairobi.

The last half of "From Now On" (from *The Greatest Showman* soundtrack) as we reentered Amarillo after a long trip.

One time as we drove into Nashville, I even dug deep down into my soul to tolerate some country music.

It's not just road trips, though. Our life comes with a soundtrack—even for our mundane, everyday tasks.

We've "Walk[ed] the Dinosaur" while wearing inflatable dinosaur costumes.

We've worked on home projects to the tune of "U Can't Touch This" by MC Hammer.

We've dance-fought to "Kung Fu Fighting" (and dealt with more than a couple minor dance-fighting-related injuries).

We've had '90s boy band sing-a-long days. And '80s rock band days. And Lecrae days. And T. Swift days.

We've sung "School's Out" every last day of school for a decade now.

We've introduced friends, family, refugees, and neighbors to spontaneous dance parties.

We've Macarena'ed. We've cha-cha'ed. We've Cupid Shuffled. We've Thriller-ed. We've Whipped. We've Nae Nae'ed. We've Let It Go.

We've stopped. We've collaborated. We've listened.

I don't often feel worthy to dole out advice, but on this subject, I do. Parents, do your best to instill a love of music in your kids.

Here's some advice from Dietrich Bonhoeffer: "Music. . .will help dissolve your perplexities and purify your character and sensibilities, and in time of care and sorrow, will keep a fountain of joy alive in you."[1] Listening to music has gotten us through some pretty rough days and added enjoyable ridiculousness to some pretty great ones. In fact, one of the turning points for our

---

1. "Dietrich Bonhoeffer Quotes," *DBonhoeffer.org*, http://www.dbonhoeffer.org/Quotes.html.

family was when we stopped merely listening to music and dancing to it and started making it ourselves. What follows is the story of how our nightly song time came to be, how we moved from listeners to singers.

In 2015, we took our family to visit a village in rural Kenya. In addition to being huge fans of raising our kids to appreciate other cultures, we wanted our family to experience a bit of life without iPods, iPads, video games, Internet, and toys. The village of Metkei, Kenya, was the perfect place for that. Metkei had very little access to electricity and total access to some of the most welcoming, friendly people in the world. While there, we visited a few churches. I knew that upon arrival, one or all of us would be expected to speak at every church we visited. I knew that because of a trip I'd taken to Kenya in 2001 when I found that out the hard way. Here's the story, straight from my blog post about the trip.

I found myself sitting in the middle of a little church in the middle of a little village in the middle of nowhere in Kenya, Africa. We were miles from electricity. The church was a small building made from sticks and mud. With the exception of a few people, everyone was standing because there was not enough room to sit. A decent-sized group of people stood outside, listening through the windows. About 45 minutes into the church service, my guide/interpreter gently elbowed me in the side.

"Hey, Josh, you're up."

Me: "Uh. . .I'm up? For what?"

Him: "You're preaching. Get up there."

Me: "Uh. Ummmm. Okay."

Apparently, when visiting a remote village in Africa, it is often customary for the guest to preach during the service. This would've been useful information to have had prior to the service. Oh well. Seeing no other option, I walked on up to the front.

I opened my Bible and began reading. Frankly, I don't even remember exactly what I read. I do remember that I initially avoided eye contact with the congregation. Why? Well, I was nervous, but there was another reason. You see, most of the women in the congregation were topless. Seriously. *National Geographic* topless. Looking up from my Bible to a room that was partially filled with smiling, topless women was a wee bit distracting. So, I planted my nose in my Bible and read. Before the interpreter had a chance to interpret anything that I said, I heard a loud voice shouting from the congregation: "BWANA ASIFIWE!" (that's Swahili for "Praise the Lord!").

Whoa. I looked behind me, thinking that perhaps Jesus had returned and I was missing it. Nope. No Jesus. Then, I looked out at the congregation. Every person in the room (both topless and clothed) was smiling at me with gigantic smiles. It dawned on me that these people—all of them—were so genuinely excited to hear a random guest speak that they couldn't contain it. So, I kept reading. Then, I talked a bit. About every 30 seconds or so, I was interrupted with "BWANA ASIFIWE!" or "ASANTE YESU!" (Thank you, Jesus!). I got more animated. I raised and lowered my voice. I waved my arms when making a point. I came out of my shell. I made eye contact. It was awesome.

I don't remember all of what I said that day, but I remember this: the content of my sermon was bad. Not theologically bad, but "bore you to sleep" bad. I'm not just saying that to be modest. It was dull as bricks. Yet, it was the most fun I've ever had preaching a sermon. I was energized because the congregation was excited. Their excitement was contagious.

The moral of the story: we've all sat through bad speakers, preachers, or presenters. Sometimes, a speaker needs a bit of help getting out of his or her shell. Be a better audience member. Liven things up a bit. Clap. Make a positive comment. Say "AMEN!" You might be surprised at how a few small comments can transform a boring speech into an energizing interaction for everyone.

The experience was, for obvious reasons, etched into my memory. But back to our 2015 trip to Kenya. This time, I made sure I was prepared to speak anywhere and everywhere we went. What I did not know is that we would also be expected to present a song along with our speech. Unfortunately, I was not prepared to sing. I was raised in the Church of Christ. Church of Christ-ers, God bless them, are ready to sing at the drop of a hat. You could walk into any group of Church of Christ people anywhere and say, "Hey, sing me a song!" and they would break out into beautiful harmony. In fact, four hours later, you'd have to be like, "Okay, guys. That's enough. You can stop singing now." My kids had basically been raised Baptist. And Baptists need a bit more prep work to be able to sing. While Baptists can put on some absolutely wonderful performances, spontaneous singing isn't really a thing. They need a guitar, a bass guitar, a piano, good lighting, nine microphones, one of those pedal boards (I still have no idea what all those contraptions are for), a choir for background vocals, an organ circa 1973, and preferably a couple of practice sessions to be able to present a song.

That said, when my family and I were invited to the front of a Kenyan church to sing, we were not ready. My kids didn't really know how to sing without instrumental accompaniment. Frantic, we brainstormed (in front of the entire congregation) and came up with only a handful of songs that all of us knew. Then I led us in the most timid rendition of "This Little Light of Mine" that has ever been performed. I don't know what level of musical performance our Kenyan audience was expecting, but I assure you that it wasn't a grown man, his wife, and a teenager singing "Don't let Satan [blows dramatically at outward-stretched index finger] it out, I'm gonna let it shine" while six kids mouthed words and tried to make themselves invisible. The von Trapps we were not. After that, we vowed we would prepare our kids to better handle public song-singing. We put together our own songbook and have been singing together as a family almost every night since we returned from that trip. (Yes, I put together a Wood family songbook, complete with an alphabetized table of contents, and that wasn't even close to being on the list of the top 10 nerdiest things I did that year.)

We'll never be the von Trapps, the Jackson 5, or that family that sang "MMMBop." My wife and kids have some skills, but my lack of vocal, instrumental, and theatrical skills is killing any chances of a family band. Sorry, family. When we returned to Kenya again in 2018, we were ready. As expected, we were asked to perform almost everywhere we visited. I was beyond proud of my kids. They rocked it.

Back to 2009 and the speaker hole in the van. For those of you whose families love music as much as ours does, you'll understand that the discovery of the gaping speaker hole was more than mere annoyance. It threatened to turn down the volume on all our adventures. So I set out to remedy the situation.

"I need to buy a new speaker to fill the hole" escalated quickly into "I should put in a TV or two to go with the new speaker." This train of thought quickly derailed into "I should redo the whole van's audiovisual system and put an Xbox in it!"

Confession: I was a fan of the show *Pimp My Ride*. I wrote to the show to see if they would tackle our van for our family of nine. For some inexplicable reason, they were not interested. I'll never forgive them or Xzibit. I decided to take matters into my own hands.

Unfortunately, reality hit quickly. As it turns out, super-fun car accessories such as Xboxes and TVs cost lots of money, and as a 30-ish-year-old father, I needed to make more grown-up decisions with my life. These two stupid facts forced me to begrudgingly scale back my plans. No amplifier. No subwoofers. No lights. No new speakers. No Xbox. No popcorn maker. No bubble machine. Ultimately, we decided on only three improvements: in-dash DVD player, ceiling-mounted TV, and replacement speaker for the speaker hole. I found the cheapest in-dash DVD player I could find and had it installed. My parents bought us a flip-down TV as a gift (thanks, Mom!). I called a local audiovisual company and got a quote for installing the TV. After throwing up in my mouth a little bit, I decided to attempt to install the TV myself. How hard could it be? I figured it would take me, Google, and YouTube a couple of hours at most. Forty-eight hours and a lot of discouraging words later, the TV was installed and hooked up to the DVD player. I felt great. I was a man. "I don't need you, *Pimp My Ride*. I don't need you, Xzibit," I thought to myself. Everything worked great!

Then, everything didn't work great. I had made one small mistake. I had spliced the wires that power the TV into the wires that power the interior lights. So the TV only worked while the door was open or while the interior lights were on. Switch off the lights = switch off the TV. Stupid. Eventually, I had a professional fix my mistake. Unfortunately, this unexpected expense effectively killed the budget for the one item on my list that mattered when I started the project: a new speaker for the side door. Don't judge me. I can't be the only one who completes projects like this, can I? The speaker hole was born.

"Why didn't you cover the hole?" you ask.

I could have glued the speaker cover back on, but I set the cover down somewhere in our house, and it was accidentally thrown away. Things like that happen a lot when you have a large family. Keys, remote controls, shoes, socks, toothbrushes, toys, and more. We've had all of them thrown in the trash or flushed at some point. Not long ago, I found a corn dog under one of our couches, a remote control in the refrigerator, and my keys in the trash. But I digress.

I suppose I could have ordered a cheap replacement speaker cover on eBay, but I didn't think of that option until I just now typed this sentence. At the time, it also seemed as though it would be less ghetto-looking to have an open speaker hole than to cover said speaker hole with duct tape or cardboard or something. God only knows what made its way into the speaker hole over the years. I didn't have the stomach to check.

Over time, I think we all got used to the speaker hole. However, it took a long time and approximately 2,576,982 uses of the sentences "TURN IT DOWN! IT'S TOO LOUD BACK HERE" and "TURN IT UP! I CAN'T HEAR IT!"

No matter. When your family is making its own music together, you don't care as much where the background music is coming from. Sure, singing together as a family was awkward at first. I had to get over my discomfort with my not-so-talented and often off-key voice being heard. But it was worth it. Now it doesn't matter as much if a speaker is missing in the door of the van—or if the entire sound system goes out. We'll keep on singing. Long live the speaker hole.

CHAPTER 3
THE SCUFF MARKS

Back to the 2018 Struggle Bus ad:

One side of the van has a yellow scuff mark on it. That's courtesy of me and a battle with a yellow concrete parking divider (I did not win). The other side of the van has a matching white scuff mark. That one is courtesy of my wife. She completes me. In related news, you know how most cars these days come equipped with a fancy backup camera? This one does not.

My wife and I have used this van for the better part of a decade. We're a lovely couple, but we sometimes inadvertently back into inanimate objects. Also, we've been forced to take a defensive driving class a few more times than the average American. That said, there are a number of other minor scratches, dents, and places where the paint is chipped on this vehicle.

I have three questions for you:

1. Have you ever taken a defensive driving class to rectify your driving sins?
2. Have you ever had the luxury of driving and parking a large van?
3. Do you have an unreasonable disdain for the phrase "She completes me"?

If you answered yes to all the preceding questions, you get me. I hope you'll read this chapter in commiserating solidarity with me.

If you answered no to the preceding questions, spoiler alert:

1. Don't judge me. I've repented of my driving sins.
2. Large vans are awful, unforgiving, beastly vehicles.
3. Hear me out before you judge me.

Before I get to the story of the infamous yellow scuff mark and my disdain for the phrase "She completes me," let's chat about defensive driving.

Have you ever taken a defensive driving class to rectify your driving sins? I have.

I don't know how the law works in other states, but the great state of Texas allows its residents to right their speeding-related driving wrongs by taking a so-called defensive driving class. My wife's and my driving records have been clean for a few years, but before that, our driving records were, well, not great. I've lost track of how many times we've sat through defensive driving classes, but it's more than seven. There was one point in our married life when my wife, my mother-in-law, and I all received speeding citations within a few days of one another. A few weeks later, we all sat together in defensive driving class in a row of shame. It was a low moment for the family. That said, when it comes to speeding-related stories, we have far more stories than we should. However, I think my favorite speeding-related story is one that ended without a citation.

Not too long after we purchased the Struggle Bus in 2009, my wife was accidentally driving a bit over the speed limit in a school zone. Out of the corner of her eye, she saw the flash of blue and red lights, and she heard the familiar siren song of impending despair. She pulled over and awaited her inevitable judgment. As the police officer approached the driver's side van window, he could, no doubt, already hear the weeping, wailing, and gnashing of teeth coming from our van. Every one of our kids—ages five, three, three, one, one, and two months at the time—were in tears. Our youngest was screaming because he was hungry. Our eldest was yelling, "OH NO! OH NO! OH NO! MOMMY'S GOING TO JAIL! THEY'RE TAKING HER TO JAIL!" Our three-year-olds were wailing at the prospect of losing their mother. Our other kids likely had no idea why they were crying but figured it was only logical to crank up the volume on their own sadness.

The police officer reached the window with an odd look of amusement and horror (he had no doubt heard our daughter screaming about prison). He peered into the van through the driver's side window, lowered his glasses, and asked the question that my wife (along with other moms of large families) is asked almost every day of the year.

"Are those all your kids?"

"Yes, they are," she replied.

"Well, ma'am. How far away do you live?" he asked.

"I live in this neighborhood. I'm just trying to get home," she replied.

"You just get home quickly and safely."

He issued no ticket or warning. He departed with a look of "Clearly you've been punished enough today."

Some days, life shows you grace in the form of a policeman. Other days, unfortunately, life rips grace away from you. Sometimes, life uses a yellow concrete barrier to punish you for your transgressions and simultaneously mark you a sinner with an unwashable yellow scuff mark—the van driver's version of a scarlet letter *A*.

Have you ever had the luxury of driving and parking a large van? It is not a vehicle of grace or forgiveness. It's a vehicle of struggle.

Parking our extended 15-passenger van has always presented us with challenges. For example, during one of our many road trips to College Station to visit our beloved alma mater, Texas A&M University, we found ourselves waiting in line to get into an on-campus parking garage. I paid, entered, and promptly hit the swinging height limit sign at the entrance. Ugh! Our van was too tall for the parking garage. On the bright side, I'm glad we discovered the issue before getting totally wedged under a concrete parking garage ceiling. What would you even do if that happened? Fortunately, I was not forced to find out. Here's to you, inventor of the swinging height limit sign. Unfortunately, though, I still had to back out of the parking garage. Do you know what's not fun? Shifting your van into park while it's at the front of a long line, exiting said van, walking to each driver's window of the seven cars behind you, and asking each driver to back up so you can back your oversized mega bus of a van out of the parking garage. Shame. Thankfully, Texas Aggies are wonderful people, and every one of them happily obliged. Gig 'em.

Of course, the van's tallness isn't usually its main problem when parking. The problems are usually due to its width and length. It is too wide for some parking spaces and too long for some parking lots. In normal-sized vehicles, there are occasions when parking requires an extra turn. Instead of a process of turn and park, it's a process of turn, reverse, turn, park. In the van, the default process is turn, reverse, turn, park. Unfortunately though, this process often becomes turn, reverse, turn, reverse, mouth the words "I'm so sorry" to anyone else in the parking lot, turn, reverse, give up hope, drive to the faraway parking land of empty spaces alongside the RVs, roadside puppy sellers, charity car wash advertisers, and the occasional fancy sports car whose driver has deemed his car too special to park alongside the peasants near the store, turn, and then double-park in two spaces.

In my effort to avoid the embarrassment of the 11-point parking process, I began to develop a bit of a radar for the best parking lots and parking spaces within these lots. I think other drivers of large vehicles develop a similar radar. The best parking spots are adjacent to the handicap-accessible spaces. Why? For one, there are usually some painted diagonal "Don't park here" stripes on the asphalt that allow enough room for my kids to violently swing the door open without risk of lowering the resale value of any car parked next to us. In most other parking spaces—spaces devoid of these painted diagonal "Don't park here" stripes—I am forced to park as close to the driver's side parking space line as I can to allow enough room on the passenger side of the van for my kids to swing the doors open or for my wife or me to wrangle the kids out of car seats and out of the van. Unfortunately, this parking arrangement only allows me about a 12-inch gap to open the driver's side door. Small car drivers don't appreciate this dilemma. Why? You, small car driver, are not a wide load. When a car is parked next to you, you can open your door all the way, casually step out of your Prius, and do a few stress-relieving I've-been-in-this-car-for-too-long stretches. You can do all that without any risk of touching or scratching the car next to you. Cherish it. I don't have that luxury. To extricate myself from my van, I have two choices.

Choice one is to crawl over the mess of kid junk that litters the Struggle Bus and exit through a passenger side door. There are risks with that option, of course. These risks primarily consist of navigating a minefield of sippy cups, fragile toys, and leftover Chick-fil-A sauce packets. I've suffered collateral damage from all three on multiple occasions.

Choice two is to contort my body like an acrobat to squeeze through the 12-inch door gap while simultaneously keeping a firm grip on the doorframe to keep it from knocking against whatever poor soul's vehicle is parked next to mine. There are also risks with this option such as buttons being ripped off clothing, strained muscles, cramps, and looking stupid to passersby. I've suffered from all four because I'm not an acrobat—a fact you'll gain a deeper understanding of in the next chapter when I lament my joy-crushing experience with P90X. My wife was once in the midst of one of these exit-the-van dances when her belt loop caught on the door-locking mechanism and broke it off. I once toppled out of the van like a circus performer. As we get older, I'm convinced that our greatest risk of injury is no longer sports or fun, adventurous activities. No, our greatest risk of injury is contorting ourselves to squeeze our way out of our van when we're parked in a tight parking spot.

Another benefit of parking in the spaces next to the handicap-accessible spaces was that our van acquired fewer door dings. You see, the drivers and passengers of cars who parked next to us had a nasty habit of door-dinging the mess out of our van's side—sometimes as I was watching. I never said anything, though. I guess I always felt as though I owed it to them. I parked too close to you, so as my penance, I allow you to therapeutically bang the heck out of my van with your door. Enjoy it. You're welcome. I only have myself and my large family choices to blame.

This brings me to the story of how the yellow scuff mark came to be.

Our church used to sponsor an event called church family vacation. Twenty or so families from the church loaded up their kids and headed to a block of rooms at the Embassy Suites hotel in Colorado Springs. We spent a couple of fun days bowling, going to the zoo, and avoiding the stupid Texas heat. On the second day, we all finished breakfast and exited the hotel as a group. Other families casually walked their normal-sized families across the street and hopped into their lovely, normal-sized, and seemingly immaculate Tahoes, Explorers, Suburbans, minivans, and the like. We herded our children over to our giant, white, eyesore of a van.

I was legitimately bummed to leave our parking spot. It was one of those luxurious spots that large van drivers dream about. There was an empty parking space on the driver's side. As such, there would be no need for a contortionist exit-the-driver's-side-van-door-without-door-dinging-the-car-next-to-me routine.

In addition to the empty parking space on the driver's side, there was no parking space on the passenger side. On the asphalt, there were some of those aforementioned painted "Don't park here" lines along with a yellow concrete parking divider. To a large van driver, this was basically the holy grail of parking spaces—even better than parking next to a handicap-accessible space. There was plenty of room for the driver and all passengers to exit. Additionally, when the kids flung the doors open, there was no room for another car to park close enough for its passengers to gaze and pass judgment upon the mid-road-trip depravity that was the van's gnarly interior.

Unfortunately, the time had come for me to part with my God-given parking space. We loaded up everyone in the van, and I begrudgingly shifted into reverse. I made a sharp turn as I backed out of the spot. SCREEEEEECH. Oops. Pole. What do you do when you have a pole nestled against the side of your van? Do you go forward? Do you go backward? Either option is going to elongate the scrape. I made a split-second decision. I chose poorly. I chose to continue backing up, leaving the now-infamous yellow scrape along the side of the van.

It would have been nice had the incident happened in a dark, empty Walmart parking lot during one of my many late-night, sleep-deprived, diaper-exploded-and-we're-out-of-diapers-angst-infused-rage drives to the store. Sure, I may have transformed like the Incredible Hulk into something resembling Dude Perfect's Rage Monster, but at least it would have happened with minimal witnesses under the cover of night. Alas, it happened in broad daylight in front of our friends. And their children. At our church family camp. Adding to the embarrassment was what I'll call the law of parent fail amplification. Here's how it works. Suppose that, hypothetically speaking, you have nine kids. You have nine of the greatest blessings in the world, but you also have nine ever-present, storytelling witnesses who view your mistakes as show-and-tell opportunities for friends, family, strangers, and basically anyone with whom they come into contact for the foreseeable future.

Kid: "Hey, Daddy! Remember when you hit that yellow pole?"
Me: "Do you mean, like, five minutes ago? Yes, unfortunately I do."
Kid: "Can I use your phone to FaceTime Nana and Grandy about it?"
Me: "No."

Kid: "It's okay. I'll just wait until we get home."
Me: "Thanks."

Shame.

We made it back to Amarillo, and my wife immediately drove the van into the first concrete barrier she could find just to make me feel better. Okay, I'm pretty sure hers was an *accidental* concrete-barrier-ramming. Either way, it did make me feel better.

Do you have an unreasonable disdain for the phrase "She completes me"? I do.

Later, as the van ad was going viral, "She completes me" was one of the most quoted lines from the post. I found this incredibly ironic. Why? Outside the world of ridiculous used car ads, "She completes me" happens to be one of my least favorite phrases. Don't hate me. Allow me to explain.

For starters, saying "you complete me" to my wife implies that, in turn, I complete her. You've only made it three chapters into this book so far, and you've probably realized that I'm too imperfect to complete anyone. Leave it to me to complete someone, anyone, and I will fail them. Probably mightily. I count on Jesus to do the completing of things.

Suppose my wife and I are in the midst of an argument. I don't get to say things like, "Hey, I complete you, I win" or "You aren't really completing me right now." I suppose I could, but it wouldn't end well. The times when our marriage has been the hardest have been the times when I've counted on my wife to do the completing—when I've relied solely on her to bring peace or stability or religion or sage parenting wisdom. I think she would say the same. Actually, she's sitting next to me as I write this. I just asked her. She agrees.

I've heard Matt Chandler use two phrases repeatedly: "Husbands make terrible gods" and "Wives make terrible gods." Truth. If my wife were to count on me to do only the things God can do—whether it's taking away her insecurity or bringing a sense of total contentment to her life or parallel parking a 15-passenger van—I will fail her. And vice versa. If I count on my wife to fix all my flaws, she isn't capable.

My wife is my favorite human on this earth, but I don't love her because she completes me in some mystical, cosmic, soul mate type of way. I love her because she has proved time and time again that she is committed to me. She works at our marriage daily. I love her because she realizes that her Pontiac Grand Prix–driving, 22-year-old fiancé, Josh Wood, was a completely different person than the 15-passenger-van-driving dad, Josh, she's married to today, and that someday, that 55-year-old Josh will be completely different from today's Josh, and she'll work to create new adventures with and love that guy, too. The excitement of our marriage hasn't been in constantly searching to renew the original spark of love felt by a couple of foolish teenagers. The older we get, the more we realize how shallow that original spark was. It isn't something to be sought after. It's simply something to happily remember. Sure, it was a great starting point, but it is a terrible destination. In our marriage, we work to create new sparks in new ways with the continually changing spouse we're each committed to. I think this is part of the reason our marriage is so fun. I'm not going to wake up one day and be like, "Who is this person, and what happened to the girl I fell in love with?" I wake up to a person I love who is changing gradually every day, just like I am.

Life isn't about finding completeness in parking spaces or human relationships. Life is about finding joy in the midst of a slew of changes and mistakes—yours, your spouse's, your kids', and your society's. Many Christian writers speak of a God-shaped hole in our hearts that nothing other than God can fill. Life is about finding completeness in God rather than seeking a feeling of completeness in things that will fail you such as perfect driving, perfect grades, perfect kids, perfect performance reviews, or perfect spouses.

CHAPTER 4
THE STUPID DOOR LINER

When you open the side doors, the rubber door liner
is detached in some places. It still does its job, but it looks stupid.

That detached door liner in the Struggle Bus did look stupid, but it did the job. You could also say that about many of the home improvement projects I've undertaken over the years. While I usually finish tasks, the end result is often more utilitarian than aesthetically pleasing. We have a friend who is quite handy with home projects. Whenever we ask for help, she is sure to remind us of her motto: "If you want it done now, call me. If you want it done right, call a professional." That's how we roll. When it comes to home projects, we sometimes opt for "done-ish now" over "done perfectly later." A similar theme runs throughout our family life. "It still does its job, but it looks stupid" could be said for all kinds of things in our world. This chapter is devoted to a few of those things: our bedroom TV, P90X, running a marathon, and last but certainly not least, my potty-training methods.

Our Bedroom TV
Occasionally after songs and prayer time and putting the kids to bed, my wife and I enjoy crashing in our bed and mindlessly binge-watching Netflix (among our favorites are *Psych* and *The Office*, in case you're curious). Originally, our bedroom TV was located on my side of the bed. Some nights, "I'll watch one episode" accidentally turned into "I just finished season 3!" If you have Netflix, you know there's a point after several episodes of binge-watching that Netflix tries to passive aggressively stop you. It arbitrarily pauses your show and presents you with this question: "Are you still watching?" We all

know what Netflix is really saying with this clever little pop-up question: "Are you seriously still watching this show? You have a family. You have work to do. You have a life. Are you sure you want to do this to yourself, you lazy sluggard?" My answer is always similar, that "2:00 a.m. is no time for judgment, Netflix! Yes, I am still watching *Friends*. I changed 74 diapers today, cleaned spaghetti sauce off the ceiling, and fished baby poop out of the bathtub. Let me be!"

Whenever I pushed my binge-watching past the point of Netflix's passive-aggressive judgment, my neck would hurt the entire next day from having it turned to the left toward our TV for, well, more hours than I care to admit. I call it "Netflix neck." Yes, I'm aware that this is one of the most ridiculous "injuries" ever. I was determined to remedy the issue, so I brainstormed. Idea number one was to permanently mount a board to the footboard of the bed and mount the TV to said board. For some reason, my wife was not on board (no pun intended) with this plan. Idea number two was to create a detachable board that could be stored under the bed along with the TV. Ultimately, idea number two was too cumbersome to be functional. Finally, I had an epiphany and developed a functional prototype. I used bungee cords to attach our iPad to the business end of our Swiffer Sweeper. Then I attached the handle of our Swiffer to the headboard of our bed. My wife walked into our bedroom to find me happily watching Netflix on an iPad that was hovering a couple feet in front my face. She was not as amazed by my brilliance as I was. Nonetheless, the two of us utilized my Swiffer-headboard-iPad contraption and binge-watched Netflix until the wee hours of the morning. Victory. It did its job, but it looked stupid.

Here's the rest of the story. Eventually, we were forced to use our Swiffer for its intended purpose. So I mounted the TV to our ceiling. Yes, our bedroom TV is mounted to our ceiling on a swivel. It does its job, but it looks stupid. Go ahead and judge me, but when we choose to binge-watch a show (which we try not to do too terribly often these days), my neck doesn't hurt the next day. It's awesome.

P90X

My wife and I decided to give the P90X fitness program a try. In case you are unfamiliar with the product, it is billed as "a revolutionary system of 12 highly intense workouts on 12 DVDs, designed to transform your body in 90 days."

I think I can safely file this decision in the overly optimistic category (like the time I said yes to dodgeball with middle schoolers, but that's another story). Here's my brief synopsis of the first three days of the program.

Day 1: We decided to start with the disc titled "Plyometrics." Tony (the leader whom I have officially declared my archenemy) pointed out that one of the guys on the video had a prosthetic leg. Assumption: if he can do it with one leg, I ought to be able to do it with two. Stupid assumption. I collapsed around 40 minutes into it. I was no longer the boss of my own legs. I realize that the following sentence isn't exactly politically correct, but I don't care. I hate that jolly one-legged man.

Day 2: I decided to go with the "Chest and Back" disc since my legs felt like Jell-O and were barely functional. My wife was initially opposed to this disc because she wanted to avoid getting a muscled-up "man back," as she so eloquently put it. I assured her that this wouldn't happen to her and warned her that it probably wouldn't happen to me, either. Apparently, each workout includes a warm-up. This warm-up included things called jump-lunges. I hate Tony. As for the rest of the workout, I again ended up sprawled on the floor—like a dead man—after semi-completing countless push-ups. Pain. So much pain. Not only was I unable to walk like a normal human, I was also unable to lift my arms to floss my teeth.

Day 3: I sifted through the discs and found a disc titled "Yoga." YES. This one had to be easy. I knew a fat guy in college who took a yoga class to meet women (didn't work). Assumption: if my chubby friend could do it, surely I could, too. Horrible assumption. Apparently, all yoga is not the same as P90X yoga. It's as if the P90X trainers thought to themselves, "By now, the people who are stupid enough to do our program probably have ridiculously sore legs, arms, and shoulders. I wonder how we can intensify that pain until our participants cry, 'OH, I KNOW! Let's make them do 90 minutes of yoga!'" I did something called a downward dog until my soul hurt. Realization 1: I am not flexible at all. AT ALL. Realization 2: yoga is not what I thought it was (a style of peaceful, calming stretching and breathing). Yoga is not peaceful at all. Yoga is designed to punish you for not being flexible. I hate yoga. I hate Tony.

I'll admit, before beginning P90X, this thought crossed my mind: "The wife might be impressed with my strength and athleticism." Wrong. Unless, of course, shouting various insults at the TV whilst lying motionless on the floor is impressive. P3X down. P87X to go. *Bring it on.*

The rest of the story: My wife and I semi-completed the remaining days of the P90X program. Intense. I can say that the program does its job, but I looked stupid.

Marathon

There are individuals in this world who are exhausting. They never follow through on commitments. You can't count on them. They seem to live their lives in constant states of drama, excuses, and annoyance. These people can't be trusted. When these people say something like, "Hey, I'm going to [insert name of some adventure]. Are you interested?" you reply, "No, thank you. I'd rather not end up alone, dead, or miserable." You avoid adventures with these people because you know that even if their plan sounds great, you'll end up exhausted or annoyed or both.

Fortunately, there are other individuals who are the opposite of the exhausters. They're generally wonderful. They follow through on commitments even if it costs them dearly. They can be trusted. When these people say something like, "Hey, I'm going to [insert name of some adventure]. Are you interested?" you blurt out, "Yes! I'm in! Wait, what was the question? What are we doing? Never mind. It doesn't matter. Let's go!" You go on adventures with these people because you know that even if you fail, somehow and some way you'll end up having a ton of fun. In 2017, a good friend of mine—who happens to be one of these good people—asked if I would be interested in running a marathon with him.

"I'm in!" I replied, without giving it a second thought.

The first week of training was a blast. I researched. I found a training plan on the Internet. I bought some sweet HOKA shoes. I bought nine flavors of gel packs, a bottle of electrolyte pills, and some Gatorade. I started a three-month trial of Apple Music and created an awesome playlist consisting primarily of songs recorded prior to 1998. Michael Jackson. Tupac. OutKast. Red Hot Chili Peppers. Metallica. AC/DC. Nostalgia was my guide. If you tossed a CD in a fire at a church youth rally in the mid-'90s, I probably had at least one song from said CD on my playlist. After work, I ran two to four miles per day. Running was a relaxing diversion from the day-to-day grind. This was going to be great!

Then weeks two through 30 came. As it turns out, training plans for marathons require you to run a lot more than two to four miles per day. A. Lot. More. Within a week, I had tried all nine gel pack flavors—all of them tasted like disappointment. A couple days later, I exhausted my supply of Gatorade and was too ~~cheap~~ frugal to spend money to buy more of the stuff. As if to add insult to injury, my music selection wasn't making me happy anymore. As it turns out, there was a reason youth pastors across America were encouraging people to toss CDs into bonfires. Tupac, while a lyrical genius, was quite a potty mouth. I cancelled my Apple Music subscription and went back to my pre-training listening regimen of sermons and audio books. No, they weren't as fun to run to, but I no longer had a nagging feeling that I was somehow disappointing Jesus.

Now that I was no longer propelled forward by expletive-infused tunes with catchy beats, my increasingly longer training runs were growing increasingly boring. In an effort to break up the monotony, I took to using my Nike app and GPS to run in shapes. Apparently, this is a thing that other people do as well (google "running in shapes" for some creative examples). First, I ran my route in the shape of a guy who had collapsed on the ground. It was a work of GPS art imitating life—or something. I ran the same route many more times, adding accessories to my GPS man—a hat one day and a failed attempt at a soccer ball another. A couple weeks later, I mapped out a way to run in the shape of GPS man playing with a yo-yo. It would require me to run across a large, undeveloped lot in the neighborhood, and that would be an added bonus (running on paved roads gets old). Unfortunately, my GPS yo-yo man run was ill-timed. As I was running the path that would create the yo-yo string from the yo-yo back up to the yo-yo man's hand, a sheriff's SUV hopped the curb about a hundred yards away and sped toward me with his lights flashing. Uh oh. A number of thoughts quickly crossed my mind.

"Is it illegal to run across this undeveloped land?"

"Am I trespassing?"

"This is totally going to mess up all my GPS hard work."

I stopped mid-stride, walked toward the oncoming SUV, took out my ear buds, and watched as the driver abruptly stopped and jumped out of his car to come at me.

"What are you up to out here?" he asked.

My eyes darted up and to the left as I pondered the absurdity of the answer that I, a grown man, was about to give to an officer of the law. "Well, you see, sir. I was running in the shape of a guy playing with a yo-yo. I had to leave the pavement over there and run through this here field because this is where the string to the yo-yo goes."

It was too much. It was too ridiculous. I couldn't bring myself to say the words I was thinking. I responded, "I was out for a run."

"Which direction did you come from?" he replied.

"The little circle drive that formed my yo-yo, right over there," I thought. But I replied (pointing north), "That neighborhood over there."

"Okay. We're looking for a suspect in the area. Have you seen anyone?" As it turned out, the police had shown up at a house nearby to bust a few drug dealers. A few ne'er-do-wells were arrested, but one feisty fella who somewhat matched my description despite being far less handsome decided to give the officers a little bit of excitement. He jumped out a window and fled on foot in my general direction. What are the odds?

Unfortunately, I hadn't seen anyone. I probably would have seen him had I not been solely focused on running the correct path for GPS yo-yo man. In any case, once the kind officer had decided that I was not the suspect he was looking for, he hopped back in his SUV and sped off. I was free, but my app had paused during my conversation with the officer. The encounter totally messed up my yo-yo string. I was able to successfully complete yo-yo man the next day without any interference from the law. (If you're curious, you can see yo-yo man in all his glory on my Instagram account from March 6, 2018.)

The remaining weeks of my training regimen proved to be devoid of criminal interference. I kept running around in ridiculous GPS shapes, but I mostly avoided plots of undeveloped land.

Then, at long last, race day arrived. I felt ready.

The first 19 miles of the Oklahoma City Marathon were actually pretty great. I felt fine. I had plenty of energy. I had read about a so-called 20-mile wall that runners hit—a mental and physical wall where many runners shut down—but I was beginning to believe it was a myth. At mile 19, I thought,

"This is great! I should have run at a bit faster pace. I guess I'm not going to hit that wall everyone talks about."

Then, just after mile 20, something changed. Bam! Wall. My brain was like, "Okay, body, you're exhausted. Let's slow down the pace, change to some upbeat music, and finish this thing." My body was like, "Nah, better not. I'm done now. Brain stupid." With bursts of starts and stops, I walk-jogged the last six miles before using the last of my energy to run across the finish line.

An overly eager race volunteer congratulated me on finishing and offered me a celebratory hamburger. Rather than accepting the burger or acknowledging his existence, I staggered a few more steps toward the loving arms of my wonderful wife and then collapsed onto the pavement, writhing in agony and finally guzzling a couple bottles of Powerade. My sweet wife helped me get to my feet and meander over to the first-aid tent where a couple of volunteers repeatedly stabbed my calves and thighs with tiny knives. In hindsight, they may have been massaging my legs rather than stabbing me. I can't be sure. I was a bit delirious. As a husband, there are moments in your married life when your wife gazes upon you with pride, longing, and a bit of lust. This was not one of those moments. She had given birth six times and handled all six births infinitely better than I was handling one road race. We both knew it. I had finished the marathon, but I looked stupid.

This past summer when our family returned to Kenya, we spent a few weeks working with some of our favorite people and one of our favorite organizations, Christian Relief Fund. Our hotel was in the city of Eldoret, home of the Kenyan Olympic training center and thus some of the best runners in the world. It felt as though every Kenyan in the area was a born runner. One evening, we found ourselves sitting around the dinner table when the topic of running came up.

"Are you a runner?" one of our Kenyan friends asked me.

Knowing my audience, I answered proudly but cautiously, "Well, I did run my first and only marathon a few weeks ago."

"Really? What was your time?" another Kenyan friend replied.

"About four hours," I said, reasonably proud.

Both of my Kenyan friends immediately and simultaneously burst into laughter as if each knew what the other was thinking. "Oh. You're not a runner! Kenyans can run it in half that time!"

We all shared a good laugh over my marathon story and how my effort paled compared to virtually every Kenyan we encountered. The moral of the story: Josh Wood = not a runner.

Potty Training

When you have a large family, there are a few phrases you find yourself saying regularly during vacations.

"Does everyone have shoes on?"

"Did everyone bring a jacket?"

"Has everyone used the bathroom?"

Each question carries a virtually identical statistical array of answers. But there's a 75 percent chance that the answer from at least one child will be no.

There's a 15 percent chance that the answer from at least one child will be a false positive because they answered yes without actually having heard the question.

There's a 10 percent chance that the answer from at least one child will be a false positive because they have somehow inexplicably mentally translated the questions as follows: "Do you or someone you know own shoes?" or "Have you ever seen an item of clothing that resembles a jacket or coat?" or "Have you used the bathroom at any point in your life?"

There's a statistically insignificant chance that the answer will be a resounding yes from all parties—including us parents.

We were in San Diego and leaving the hotel to head to the beach. "Has everyone used the bathroom?"

"Yes," they all assured us.

We arrived at the beach and staked out a spot near the lifeguard station— because sharks. Approximately 27 seconds after we had everything set up, one of our four-year-olds (almost five) said the dreaded words, "Mommy, I need to go potty."

"Poop or tee-tee?" I replied.

"Just tee-tee," he said.

"Son, you're in luck. That's the ocean out there. We can't do this just anywhere, but this time you can go out into the ocean and tee-tee in there."

He looked at me a bit awkwardly, so I reassured him. "It's okay this time. No poop, though. Just tee-tee out in the ocean."

Off he went. Truthfully, I've always been a bit uncomfortable with the whole idea of relieving yourself in the ocean. Since you're already judging me anyway, here's the deal. I'm generally against the idea of my kids doing their business anywhere except a toilet. It feels wrong. However, on that day, I was more against the idea of getting up from my comfy beach spot to find a public restroom that would be generous enough to open its doors to a kid who is clearly still in the learning-to-aim stage of bathroom usage. Sorry, California. Sorry, Pacific Ocean.

As my four-year-old made his way down to the ocean (10 to 20 yards away), I checked on our other kids. A few seconds later, I shifted my gaze back to my four-year-old to make sure he wasn't going too far out into the ocean. He wasn't. He was standing there, barely ankle-deep in the water, with his swim trunks dropped to his feet—baring it all in front of God and everyone. He was simultaneously mooning the beachgoers behind him whilst putting on a fountain show for the ocean-dwellers in front of him. "NOOOOOOOO!" Alas, I was too late. The deed was done. He had peed in the ocean. He yanked his swim trunks up and happily frolicked out into the ocean. Rookie mistake, Dad. I should've been more specific. Sorry, La Jolla beachgoers.

My potty-training method—it did its job, but it looked stupid.

Whether it's projects, personal development, or parenting, I sometimes look stupid. I prefer practice now over perfection later. I've decided that living a life where you do stuff and sometimes look stupid trumps a life where you do nothing and look distinguished. That hasn't always been my mantra, though. My nature is quite the contrary. My personality wants to be distinguished. It wants to be perfect. It wants to not look stupid. Fortunately, God gave me a wife who loves whimsy and trying new things and breaking routines and meeting new people and creating grand adventures. I tell her all the time that if not for her, I would be an eccentric, antisocial workaholic who was forever planning and never acting. My wife's personality is ready, fire, aim. My personality is ready, aim, aim, aim, aim, aim, aim, aim, aim until I find a reason not to fire. Fortunately, she's taught me a valuable lesson. Sometimes, life is better when you take chances and do stuff—even though sometimes you look stupid.

CHAPTER 5
THE AUTOMATIC DOOR LOCKS

The van came equipped with automatic door locks. Unfortunately, they no longer work. Somehow, something got reversed and the locking motor ran without ceasing until the button was pressed and held down. Rather than taking the van to a repair shop like a normal person, I duct taped the button down to keep the motor from running. At some point the duct tape failed and the motor ran until it eventually burned up or something. Anyhow, the automatic door locks don't work. Each door must be locked and unlocked manually. Duct tape is not included.

I know that many of you vehicle owners strut around pushing your remote lock-unlock buttons all willy-nilly as if such things were an inalienable human right. You don't appreciate the luxury. You've probably never even thought about the magical gift of doors that automatically lock and unlock at the push of a button. Well, cherish it, my friends. Cherish it.

Okay, okay. In the grand scheme of things, living a life without automatic locks in the Struggle Bus wasn't that big of a deal, but it was perpetually annoying. Why? I'm glad you asked.

For a time, none of the little kid fingers in our family were capable of unlocking the van doors manually. Generally, of course, that was a good thing. However, suppose a child happened to push the lock into the locked position. The get-kids-out-of-the-van process instantly became more complicated because the key to the ignition doubled as the key to unlock the door. In order to extricate children from the vehicle, we had to turn the car off, put down anything we were holding, and use the key to manually unlock the door. You may be thinking to yourself, "What's the big deal, Josh? It sounds like the door locks are doing their job well." The problem: There is apparently some sinister force that lies dormant until just after the van doors shut. Then said sinister force compels every child we have under the age of eight to do everything in his or her power to press the little lock button into the locked position. Every time.

Allow me to paint a picture for you. If you have ever been on a road trip with multiple kids, you will feel our pain. When any of our sons say, "I need to go potty," he doesn't mean "Excuse me, Mom and Dad. I am feeling the need to use a restroom. If it doesn't inconvenience you, please stop at the next available establishment that houses an adequately maintained restroom." He means that he needs to go potty right at that very moment. Worse, he sometimes means that he's already going a little bit. If any of the children pressed down the lock, there would be no quick way to open the door. If I were driving, there would be no way for me to leave the car running while Careese ran the potty-goer into a gas station bathroom. The whole process took an extra 15 to 30 seconds: turn off the van, get out, sprint around to the side door, and unlock the door before sprinting off to whatever gas station bathroom had the misfortune of our presence. I'll let you guess how many times this additional 15 to 30 seconds rendered the process too slow to avoid disaster. Hint: our van did not smell like roses. Worth noting: this lock issue played a dastardly role in the forthcoming chapter's vomit struggles.

Parenting is an adventure that is full of challenges like this, right? The simplest of tasks often become complicated in ways that take you just beyond your wits' end. Sometimes it's a locked door when a child needs to use a bathroom. Sometimes it's a lost shoe when you're late for church. Sometimes it's an overflowing toilet two minutes before the start of a party you are hosting. Sometimes it's a post-bedtime cry of "Mommy!" or "Daddy!" when you're trying to catch up on laundry. Rest and relaxation are perpetually beyond your grasp.

Not long after my wife graduated from Texas A&M with her degree in education, we had our first child. Though she puts her degree to use almost every day while homeschooling our kids, she's been a stay-at-home mom ever since. Knowing how isolating that can be, we made a deal early in our marriage. Every year she takes a trip with some girl friends for a few days while I stay home with the kids. As a part of the deal, I don't get to blow the budget while she's gone. In other words, I can't take the kids out to restaurants for every meal or fill our time with mini golf or bowling or movies. It's a good annual time to reconnect with her day-to-day life. It helps me empathize and reminds me why I love her. At no time in my life are parenting challenges—and a feeling of relaxation being perpetually beyond my grasp—more prevalent than during my wife's annual girls' trip.

On one such trip, my wife was visiting some friends in the faraway land of Austin, Texas. I stayed behind with our kids (ages six, four, four, two, two, and one at the time). We went through the normal bedtime routine on Saturday night. We read Bible stories (translation: I read Bible stories, two kids listened, four kids ran around like lunatics and took turns jumping on and off the beds while I yelled things like, "Hey! Calm down! We're learning about Jesus over here!"). After Bible story time, we had prayer time. Prayer time took forever because my six-year-old was in an adorable phase where she prayed for everything in sight until I interrupted and said, "Amen!"

"Thank you, God, for carpet. And thank you, God, for beds. And thank you, God, for hair. And thank you, God, for blankets. And thank you, God, for the Wiggles. And thank you, God, for the sky. And thank you, God, for bugs. And thank you, God, for my shoe. And thank you, God, for the ceiling."

"Amen!"

Once prayer time was over, I took the kids to their beds, one by one.

Careese was returning the next day, so I had planned to spend the remainder of the evening making the house look as if it hadn't been completely destroyed in her absence. Cleaning the house while kids slept should have been a time-consuming but simple task. Nope. Not long after the kids were all in bed, I heard the sound of crying coming from one of my four-year-old daughters' room.

"Daddy!"

I stopped cleaning and walked in to check on her.

She was sitting up in her bed with her eyes half-closed. "Daddy, there's a flower in my nose."

Clearly, she'd been dreaming. I laughed a little at her adorably sleepy self and asked, "How did a flower get in your nose?"

Her: "The wand got it in there."

Me: "So a magical nasal flower wand implanted a flower in your nose?"

She gave me a confused stare.

"Where is the magic wand now?" I asked.

Her: "In the drawer in the playroom."

In the drawer in the playroom. That struck me as an oddly specific fact for her to remember from a dream. I was expecting a different answer. I was expecting an answer that would have been more in line with other dream stories she had told me in the past—perhaps an answer involving a unicorn or a talking kitten or something. I was still convinced that she had been dreaming, but the imaginary flower in her nose was clearly upsetting her. So I decided to fake-examine her nose and fake-extract the imaginary flower so she would go back to sleep.

"Let's go back to sleep. I'll look and see if there is a flower in your nose."

I proceeded to perform a fake, nasal-flower extraction. During the faux extraction, I noticed that her nose was red and bleeding a little.

Ugh! Surely there wasn't actually a flower in her nose, right? I took her into the bathroom and used a flashlight to peer into her nostrils. Sure enough, at the very back of her nasal passage was the glimmer of a shiny, flower-shaped object. Then it all clicked. She and her sisters had attended a birthday party and received little wands as a party favor. The little wands had tiny sequin flowers on the ends. NOOOOOOOOOOOO!

"Did you shove a flower wand up your nose?" I asked.

"Yes," she replied matter-of-factly.

Me: "WHY?"

Her: "I don't know."

My daughter, for some inexplicable reason, had, in fact, shoved a wand up her nose and lodged a shiny sequin flower up in her nasal cavity. Fantastic.

At first I thought she might be able to blow it out. Have you ever tried to teach a four-year-old to blow air out of his or her nose? It's surprisingly difficult, especially when you're in the midst of a stressful situation. I covered her mouth and non-obstructed nostril and told her to blow out. She inhaled.

"NO! WRONG WAY!" I gasped.

She cried. I calmed down.

"I'm sorry. Daddy just doesn't want the flower to go farther up your nose. Sweetheart, you're sucking in air rather than blowing it out. Try to make the air go the other way. Out. Not in. Out. Not in." (Picture me making ridiculously overly exaggerated nose-blowing faces.)

After numerous attempts at nose blowing, the flower had moved farther up into her nasal cavity where it was barely visible.

I figured that my next best option would be to attempt to extract the shiny object with a pair of tweezers. I was starting to panic a bit. I could see the writing on the wall. If tweezers didn't work, my next stop would be the emergency room. I would be forced to wake up all the kids and load them into the van for a fun-filled adventure to the emergency room. Dragging six sleep-deprived kids ages six and under to the emergency room sounded like a fate worse than death—both for the kids and for the emergency room. In hindsight, there were, of course, more options available to me than tweezers or the emergency room. My wife would have calmly and rationally thought of all of them. Unfortunately, I wasn't exactly thinking clearly, calmly, or rationally. I searched for tweezers. Alas, no tweezers were to be found.

It was getting later, and I was growing more desperate. Fortunately, the other kids were soundly asleep in their beds. I told my flower-nosed daughter to sit tight on the couch while I ran to our neighbor's house and asked to borrow some tweezers. Most neighbors ask to borrow normal things like a cup of sugar or some eggs. Not me. I needed a pair of tweezers to pluck a sequined flower out of my daughter's nose. Sorry, neighbors. After successfully borrowing tweezers, I positioned a couple of flashlights for optimal nostril illumination and attempted the floral extraction. No luck. The flower was too deep, and I was too worried about injuring my daughter should she make any sudden movements.

I weighed my options. I didn't see any way around it. The emergency room beckoned. Ugh! I decided to carry my daughter with me to the neighbor's house to see if they would be so kind as to watch the kids while I embarked on the undoubtedly lengthy emergency room adventure. After explaining the situation, my neighbor's daughter headed to our house to babysit. The three of us adults decided to use the tweezers and take one last stab (no pun intended) at the flower extraction before I took my daughter to the emergency room. We took turns playing a disturbing, real-life version of the classic board game Operation. One of us held a flashlight. One of us held my daughter's head down and nose open. One of us wielded the tweezers. To her credit, my daughter handled the situation like a champ. She lay calmly on the table and finally figured out how to blow air out of her nose rather than suck it in.

After quite a few nose blows, the object moved into tweezer range.

"Got it!"

I pulled out a shiny metallic flower—about the size of the head of an eraser—and held it up like a trophy for all the world to see. There was much rejoicing.

The moral of the story: avoid magical-nasal-flower wands at all cost. They are horrible toys.

You parents out there understand, right? When kids enter the family picture, simplicity disappears. "Me time" is no longer a thing. Well, maybe it is, but it's usually ill-gotten me time, either by pretending to be asleep until your spouse gets up with a crying child or hiding out eating candy in the darkened confines of your closet (both scenarios are purely hypothetical, of course). Many days, you see the light at the end of the parenting tunnel. You can sense it coming. You crave it. You're about to collapse into your recliner and watch some football. You're about to get some projects accomplished after the kids go to bed. You're about to put the kids down for a nap and read a book. Then, just as you reach the end of the proverbial tunnel, you discover that there is no light there. Instead of the light of relaxation, there's nothing but shade—like your toddler holding a Sharpie marker without the lid on it. Or there's a wall covered in grape jelly. Or there's a toilet clogged with dog food. Or there's a locked van door and a disgustingly wet van seat. Or there's a shiny object at the back of your kid's nasal cavity.

When people find out we have nine kids, we often hear this: "I don't know how you do it." What some people mean by that phrase is this: "That sounds awful. Have you lost your mind? Good luck with that." They see the chaos. They see the lack of simplicity. They see the jelly-covered wall. They see the exhaustion. Sure, there are times when parenting is awful, but it's often awful in the best kind of way. It's often an adorable awfulness.

Of course, most of the time parenting isn't awful. It's wonderful. Children really are a blessing from the Lord. For every Sharpie-ed wall, we've had countless "Daddy's a superhero!" or "Momma, I snuggle you? or "Daddy, I love you most!" or "Momma is my favorite Momma!" For every grape-jellied surface, we've had far more breakfasts in bed, cleaning-the-house-for-Momma-and-Daddy days, thank-you-for-being-my-Momma-and-Daddy notes, and all sorts of other unsolicited random acts of love and kindness. For every planned time of rest that has been interrupted with kid-related chaos, we've had far more begin with kid-related happiness. Sisters reading to brothers. All nine kids playing board games or basketball or card games together. Older siblings teaching younger siblings to count or read or play a game. Sisters singing duets. Brothers having dance-offs. Countless family-wide spontaneous dance parties and sing-alongs.

Sure, relaxation feels as if it's perpetually just beyond our reach, but big family life is never boring. It's exciting. It's adventurous. It's adorable. It's hilarious. If laughter leads to a longer life, parents of large families may be tired, but they are probably close to being immortal.

I think one of the keys to parenting in any sized family is to embrace the crazy. Cherish the good times and write down the crazy times for future reading. Your older self will likely find the exhausting times to be funnier in hindsight than your current self does in the present. Embrace the imperfection and appreciate the story that you get to be part of. Sure, the door locks to my van don't work right and my child's brain thinks shoving a wand up her own nose seems like a good thing to do, but I can't imagine living in a world where everything worked correctly and kids always made intelligent decisions. I'd get more sleep in this mythical land, but I'd miss out on most of my favorite stories. That would be a shame, because, as you can probably tell, I love stories.

CHAPTER 6
THE GHOST OF VOMIT PAST

We're a family of 11. Every one of our children has thrown up in this van at some point in the past decade—most notably, on this trip: http://www.joshwoodtx.com/college-station-2015/. We have had the van detailed a couple times since then (shout out to Xtreme Auto Re-Styling Center for tackling a level of depravity unrivaled in the world of passenger transport.) The van is clean now, but it will probably always be inhabited by the ghost of vomit past.

Prepare yourself. Here's the story of our trip in the Struggle Bus to College Station in 2015—the trip that spawned the ghost of vomit past.

Day 1. Friday. We arrived in College Station and spent the day hanging out and catching up with our favorite college kid, Mary. Later that night, all the girls headed out to Midnight Yell. For you non-Aggies out there, Midnight Yell is—and I want to be careful not to overstate this—one of the greatest college football traditions of all time (google it). I stayed behind at the hotel with the boys. At about 1:00 a.m., I woke up to the always-jarring sound of the cry of our two-year-old. I looked over as his cry transformed into projectile vomit. All over his bed. All over his pillow. All over the floor. All over him. All over pretty much everything in a five-foot splash zone. Fantastic. I had just finished cleaning up when Careese arrived. Judging by the look on her face, the aromatic mix of musty hotel room and death slapped her as soon as she opened the door. "Hmmmm. So how'd everything go here?" she said as she glanced at the repulsive mountain of sheets, laundry, and towels.

"Could've been better," I replied.

Day 2. Saturday. Happily, our two-year-old seemed to be feeling better. We spent the day supporting the local economy. You're welcome, College

Station. That night, three of us joined Mary in the student section at the game (A&M vs. Auburn). Fittingly, our Aggie offense metaphorically vomited all over the field.

Despite the horrible performance, we really enjoyed the game. New Kyle Field is absolutely amazing. Afterward, the girls dropped me off at our hotel before they headed back to Mary's house to do cooler stuff than hanging out at our hotel. Cooler stuff ended up being watching and singing along to Disney's *Mulan* with a bunch of college kids. Well played, Mary's college friends. Late that night, one of our eight-year-olds informed us that his stomach was hurting. Uh oh. We positioned him within a few steps of the bathroom and handed him a small trash can.

"Please do your best to throw up in the toilet. If you don't think you can make it to the toilet in time, try your best to use this trash can. Do you understand?" we pleaded.

"Yes," he said.

"If you feel like you're going to throw up, what should you do?" we asked.

"Go to the potty or use the trash can," he answered.

"Perfect," we replied.

One minute later, our queasy little blonde volcano erupted. Those of you with kids know where his vomit went. Not in the toilet. Not in the trash can. Everywhere else.

Fantastic. After we'd cleaned and comforted him, we put on our game faces. As a parent, there are moments in life when you toss aside your need for sleep, your dignity, your pride, and your sense of self-worth to bare-handedly clean the unholy mess of junk that was just created by your offspring. This was one of those moments. After the deed was done, we tried to get some sleep. It wasn't to be. 'Twas a night filled with more eight-year-old vomiting with a side of vomit from our six-week-old. Fortunately, our littlest human only spewed once and was okay for the remainder of the trip.

So little sleep. So many showers. So much collateral damage.

Day 3. Sunday. We were exhausted, but those of us who hadn't contracted the plague dragged ourselves to church and then lunch, which went well (the restaurant Fuego rules, by the way). We were still exhausted, but we were now 12 hours vomit-free and feeling more optimistic about the prospect of our survival. Mary's awesome roommate had volunteered to go over to campus with us and take family pictures, so off we went. Despite the unusual crankiness of our kids (I'm sure due to stomach issues and prolonged exposure to the angst-infused cloud of stank in our hotel room), we had a good time roaming the A&M campus for an hour or two and taking tons of pictures (thanks, Mary's roommate!).

After pictures, we said our good-byes to Mary before dropping her off at country western dance class. Then we headed out for a quick dinner with her roommate before heading out of town.

Things went downhill for the Wood family from there.

We were enjoying our dinner when, you guessed it, more vomit. Our other eight-year-old utterly desecrated a solid six-square-foot area of our dining establishment. We again rolled up our sleeves and tossed aside our dignity. My wife informed an employee what had happened and asked for some cleaning supplies.

"Ew, gross! That's disgusting," the employee said as she turned her back and walked off.

Thanks for your help, lady. Fortunately, another employee overheard the conversation and ran to grab a mop. After everything was cleaned up, we hung our heads in shame and departed the restaurant.

We had made plans to stay the night at a friend's house in Dallas. Our kids, who are fantastic little travelers, said they were all feeling well enough to try to make the three-hour drive there. So off we went. Good-bye, College Station.

Fifteen minutes into the drive, our nine-year-old informed us that her tummy didn't feel well. Uh oh. We stopped for a minute on the side of the road. Once the nausea had subsided and she gave us the all clear, we handed her a paper bag (just in case) and continued on.

Two minutes later, BLLLAAAARRRGGGGHHH. The only item in our van within spit-shot of her mouth that remained dry was the inside of her just-in-case paper bag. Fantastic. We drove as quickly as we could to the nearest gas station and sped into one of the only parking spots available. To our right and left was a gang of chain-smoking, skull-tattooed, unkempt-bearded, cussing, angry-looking bikers. They looked pretty gnarly, but I wasn't too afraid of them. For one thing, I saw one of the dudes pull a Hello Kitty jacket out of his biker satchel and put it on underneath his black leather jacket. I don't have any facts to back up this assumption, but I'm betting that Hello Kitty is in the top three least-worn brands for thugs or robbers. And even if Hello Kitty jackets are a ruse that gnarly bikers use to lull their victims into a false sense of security, it's not like we had anything of value on us.

"Sure, take our ebola-covered Mickey Mouse DVDs, Mr. Hard-Core Biker Guy. While you're at it, go ahead and take our vomit van. Resale value is a solid $8 at this point. You're welcome."

We salvaged what items we could by rinsing them off and shoving them into trash bags. (Shout out to Sanjay, the empathetic gas station worker. Thanks for the bags, kind sir.) We threw away the rest. Midway through our roadside hazmat clean-up, my wife took off running into the bathroom. The vomit demons had taken her. Much to her credit, she made it to a toilet. Our missing-the-toilet-or-anything-else-that-might-be-easy-to-clean-up streak came to an end. I love her.

Back on the road. At this point, our van smelled, well, worse than anything you can possibly imagine. We passed out bags to everyone in preparation for the inevitable. We made it another 10 minutes. BLUGHHAAARRRBBBLLLL! Down went our 11-year-old. She made it all in her bag. Our vomit-somewhere-that-is-contained-and-easy-to-clean-up batting average was improving. We were now somewhere around .200 for the trip. Hooray! We stopped at the nearest place with a bathroom, threw up a few more times, and hopped back in the vomit mobile for the remainder of our fun-filled adventure to Dallas. At this point, one of us had the thought, "Oh no! What if we contaminated Mary? She has an exam tomorrow!" We shot her a quick text to fill her in on our rapid demise and see how she was doing. She replied that she was praying for us and felt okay at the moment. Phew.

About 20 minutes later, the violent and unforgiving plague took down our 10-year-old. We were dropping like flies. She, too, successfully used her bag. Moral victory.

Another gas station. Another cleanup. Then we got back on the road. Eight of us had now gone down. The only three left standing were our six-year-old, Mary, and I. Solidarity.

A few minutes later, we got a text from Mary with only one character: a yellow, vomiting emoticon. Down she went. And then there were two.

Not long after that, I began to feel the drums of war raging in my own stomach. My time had come. The end was nigh. We pulled over at the next gas station. By this time, the kids knew the drill. Wash up, discard the barf bags, prepare new barf bags, hydrate, and pray. I turned over driving duties to Careese. She was and will continue to be the strongest of us. On a bright note, we were all becoming quite proficient at hitting our barf bag targets. I applauded our kids accordingly. We were now a couple hours into our drive to Dallas, and we weren't even halfway there. We called to cancel our plans to stay at our friends' house, citing the inevitable doom that would befall them, their household, and all things they hold dear. Then we all loaded back into the van. "Gas station break number 87,462 is over, kids. Everyone back to the vomit comet!"

After discussing a number of less-than-ideal hotel options, we decided to see if we could make it to the south side of Dallas. We figured, worst-case scenario, we could find some tiny motel if our plight continued to worsen. Or we'd all die together on the side of the road after contaminating and subsequently ending the world as we know it—like patient zero in *World War Z*.

We carried on, frequently stopping to discard barf bags, clean up, rehydrate, and pull ourselves together. Our kids and their mommy had amazingly good attitudes, considering the circumstances. I felt more like Clark Griswold when he sort of lost his mind and sawed off the newel post in a fit of maniacal rage-laughter.

We all just wanted to make it to Dallas.

Blessedly, one by one, our kids started falling asleep, and the vomiting diminished.

At last, sometime late at night or very early morning, we arrived at a lovely Holiday Inn Express south of Dallas-Fort Worth. I walked in and saw lots of "Pardon our mess, we're under construction" signs. I thought to myself, "Well, if you aren't already a mess, you're about to be." We carried everyone up to our rooms, put everyone in bed, and then crashed.

Day 4. Monday. It was a day of miracles. Miracle #1: we all slept until at least 8:00 a.m. That was a miracle for a lot of reasons—not the least of which is that, as parents of nine, that *never* happens, not even when everyone is healthy and put to bed in their own beds. Not when we say things like, "Do not come to our bed tonight unless it is an emergency; we have to get some sleep!" *Never* happens.

Miracle #2: some of us were able to eat breakfast. After breakfast, we all took showers. Three hours of showers later (not that much of an exaggeration), we all hopped into the van for the remaining six-hour drive back to Amarillo. You would think that a night of airing out in the breeze would make the van smell better. You would be wrong. But then came Miracle #3: no one vomited on the way home. None of us felt great, but the vomit streak had apparently come to an end. After a few short, non-vomit-related stops, we arrived in Amarillo. We all rejoiced and said a prayer as we pulled into the driveway. We were survivors.

And that, my friends, is the story of our trip to College Station. Yes, our Aggies got destroyed by Auburn. Yes, our hotel room, van, and a number of tiny bathrooms got destroyed by us. Yes, there's probably one of those "Do not serve these people" pictures of us up at the Econo Lodge in College Station. Sorry, Econo Lodge. Yes, we probably ruined Mary's nice friends' dreams of having a large family. No, we were neither physically nor emotionally able to fully appreciate the greatness of College Station cuisine—Freebirds, Blue Baker, or Fuego.

But we are all survivors.

What's the moral of this story? Well, here are a few:

1. There is apparently something magical about staying at Holiday Inn Express.
2. If you own a car-detailing business, wear gloves. Also, up charge for vomit vans. Also, wear a mask. Also, don't be afraid to exercise your right to refuse service to anyone.
3. If the Wood family says, "Hey, we've got an extra seat in our van if you want a ride to [insert name of place]," you should probably say no.

On a more serious note, there was one more life lesson that this experience reinforced. It's okay to not be okay.

If your family, like ours, consists primarily of humans, perhaps you've experienced similar struggle-vomit-bus-worthy vacations or experiences. I think there are times in all our lives when we spend hours, days, weeks, or even months developing the perfect plan for something—a vacation, a career move, a significant purchase—only to have said plan destroyed by projectile vomit. We build spreadsheets. We chart courses on maps. We itemize budgets. We gather enough information on [insert large purchase item here] to teach a college-level [insert large purchase item here] 101 class. We create Pinterest boards for days. Then, just as the plan is on the brink of success, vomit—literal or metaphorical—happens. Plans are ruined. Dreams are turned into nightmares. Hopes are crushed. Spreadsheets are rendered useless. Hashtags abruptly change from #nailedit to the ironic version of the same. It's part of being human in a broken world. The question, though, is how do we react when vomit happens?

There was a time in my life when I thought my job as a Christian was to fake my way through vomit-destroyed plans with a cheery disposition and a steady deployment of out-of-context, misquoted Bible verses.

Stranger: "Hey, it looks like you're covered in vomit. Anything I can do to help?"

Me: "No, thanks! I'm great because God works all things for the good of those who love him, so sayeth Romans 8:28!"

Stranger: "Are you sure, man? It looks like you're on the brink of a mental collapse rivaling Clark Griswold when he found out his Christmas bonus consisted of a membership to the Jelly of the Month Club."

Me: "Of course I'm sure! I'm great! God has plans to prosper me and not harm me according to Jeremiah 29:11."

Stranger: "Really? Because it sort of looks like the universe had plans to harm you and has enacted said plan with crippling accuracy."

Me: "'Yea though I walk through the valley of the shadow of death, God is with me. I will fear no evil!' Psalm 23:4" (KJV).

Stranger: "If you could see yourself right now, you'd be afraid of evil. Do you want my help or not?"

Me: "No, thanks! 'To live is Christ, and to die is gain!' Philippians 1:21."

Stranger: "Well, good luck with that."

Here's the deal. Humans love authenticity more than just about anything else on the planet. The stench of fakeness is more powerful than the stench of vomit. Realness and vulnerability smell great. Authenticity draws people in. Inauthenticity repels people. That's probably why Jesus, who has always been in the business of drawing people in, levied some of his harshest words against the religious people he referred to as whitewashed tombs. Clean, filtered, blessed on the outside, dead on the inside. Props to Jesus. He was really good at metaphors.

During our College Station vomit trip and during more serious challenges we've faced in life, I've learned that it's okay to not be okay. Sometimes we're the Good Samaritan, but far too often we morph into some masochistically fake version of the robbed and beaten man, rejecting the help of all who pass by in a foolhardy attempt to make the world think we've got our lives together. I'm a continually reforming Pharisee. I've most certainly missed out on friendships in the past by pretending everything was okay when everything wasn't okay. "How's life?" a friend asks. "Good," I reply, covered in metaphorical (or sometimes literal) vomit. People don't want to be friends with me when I'm a faker. I don't blame them.

"Need some help?" asks the Good Samaritan as he draws near to my bloodied and battered section of the gutter on the side of the road.

"Nah, I'm good! 'To live is Christ, to die is gain!'" I respond, never lifting my eyes from my phone screen because I'm busy whitewashing my Instagram account with the right filter, angle, quote, and hashtag.

It's okay to admit we need help. Did you know that allowing people to help you has been scientifically proven to cause those people to like you more? It's known as the Ben Franklin Effect. I would be happy to poorly explain it here and quote the related scientific studies, but I'll let you google it.

> Next to grace, I bet God thinks making us need each other was one of His best ideas.[1]
>
> —Bob Goff

Had I not been in a rush, I'm confident that Sanjay (the helpful gas station attendant who made a cameo appearance in our College Station road trip story) and I could have built a beautiful friendship. His ability and willingness

1. Bob Goff, *AZQuotes*, https://www.azquotes.com/quote/811615.

to help us in our time of need connected us. Actually, I can't think of a single friendship in our family's life that hasn't been forged in the fire of authenticity, the igniter and fuel of friendship.

Struggling with a toddler? Tell someone. Struggling in your marriage? Tell someone. Struggling with an addiction? Tell someone. Struggling with depression? Tell someone. Heck, tell me. josh@joshwoodtx.com. Don't make the mistake of becoming a whitewashed, vomit-covered, or #blessed tomb. It's okay to admit you're not okay.

CHAPTER 7
THE AIR CONDITIONER

The automatic windows work! This is good because the air conditioner
does not. Well, it sort of works and sort of doesn't. It works fine until you
accelerate past 45 miles per hour. After that, the gas pedal essentially functions as
an on/off switch for the air conditioner. Accelerate = AC off. Decelerate = AC on.
I don't understand why. But, then again, as you've probably gathered by now,
I don't understand most things about cars.

"Dad, can we slow down so we can cool off? It's hot back here." It's a sentence that shouldn't have to be said.

Within days of posting the ad on Craigslist, I had a surprising number of messages from wonderful people across the country suggesting possible fixes for the air-conditioning issue. The most common suggested fix: repair the vacuum line. Several do-gooders went so far as to message me with instructions to fix it.

Step one: Locate the vacuum line.

You might think that locating a vacuum line—a line that had been described to me in multiple messages—would be the easiest step of the fix the air conditioner process. You would be wrong. For starters, I had only recently become aware that vans had things called vacuum lines.

I opened the hood of the van. None of the lines looked like what had been described to me. Also, none of the lines were labeled Dyson or Hoover. Also, I had no idea how to locate the line that sucked the most. Google and I went to work. Together, we located the elusive vacuum line. It was conveniently located behind a really hot thing, a couple of pretty sharp things, and a lot of incredibly dirty things that coated my hands in some other-worldly, unwashable, black, greasy substance. (I'm pretty sure it's the same substance found in a baby's first diaper, but I can't be sure.)

Step two: Detach the panel under the dash on the interior passenger side of the van. Once detached, locate the point at which the vacuum line is accessible from the inside of the van.

I felt pretty good about myself as I detached the panel with ease. Then I peered inside. I suppose I was hoping to open the panel to find a singular wire clearly labeled vacuum line. Nope. Tons of unlabeled wires. I might as well have been staring at the wiring of a space shuttle. The proverbial writing appeared on the Chick-fil-A sauce-stained van wall: "You have been weighed. You have been measured. You have been found wanting."

I reattached the panel, figuratively washing my hands of the matter and literally washing my hands with industrial-strength grease destroyer, and left the problem to the next owner to fix. Sometimes I'm a quitter like that.

After reading this much of this book, you may be surprised by this: quitting is not something that comes naturally to me. Quitting is hard. I was raised in an anti-quitting generation. In fact, my entire generation hates quitting. We canonized the phrase "Winners never quit, and quitters never win."

In our youth, we didn't quit. We forfeited lunches, dinners, hours of sleep, and the respect of society to defeat all nine levels of Mario Brothers and rescue Princess Peach. We didn't quit until Bowser was vanquished.

In our teens, we didn't quit. We brought our anti-quitting attitude into the world of sports. Our parents had to invent a thing called "run rule" because our never-quit mantra was making our games too long. Suppose the score of a baseball game was 32–0 in the bottom of the first inning. Not one of the players thought, "Well, the other team is crying, and it's getting late. I guess we should wrap this up and all go home." Heck no. The merciless players of my generation thought, "I wonder how much the other team will cry when we get to 100? It's a good thing we have eight more innings!"

In our early adulthood, we didn't quit. There are many examples, but I'll leave you with just one. A company called America Online gave out free 30-day trial CDs to entice customers to try out their dial-up Internet service. Did we quit our free Internet access after 30 days and start paying a normal rate? Heck no. We used piles of free, 30-day trial CDs—one after the other— for years of free Internet access.

Now that we've exited the world of young adulthood and are entering the world of legit adulthood, we still hate quitting. Look in our closets and you'll find at least one item of clothing from our high school or college days— that was 20-plus years ago. If our 18-year-old selves wore Adidas shoes, our 40-year-old selves are also probably wearing Adidas shoes. We take every opportunity to quote *Friends*, which debuted in 1994. My 20-year high school reunion was in 2018. There was not a single person in attendance who couldn't quote every lyric of "Ice Ice Baby." We were and are per-sis-tent. We don't let things go. We don't quit things. Not only do we hate quitting, but we loathe others telling us to quit. When Netflix interrupts our binge-watching with the pop-up message "Are you still watching [insert name of show here]?" my entire generation will keep watching—whether we want to or not—out of pure spite. No one tells us when to quit.

Life has taught me a valuable lesson, though. Persistence doesn't always pay. Persistence has led a number of my generation to a sad, pasty, energy-drink-infused life of video gaming domination that is being lived out in the confines of their parents' basements.

"Winners never quit, and quitters never win" is, in fact, a big, fat lie. Winners quit stuff all the time. For example, winners quit pretty much all stuff that happened in their parents' basements.

Winners at life are often the best quitters. Take, for example, Winston Churchill. I'll use him as an example because (1) his "Never Give In" speech epitomized my generation's winners-never-quit mantra, and (2) he helped defeat the Nazis, which qualifies him as a winner at life. Churchill quit many things, even things he was really good at. For example, his typing skills were far superior to the typing skills of the typist he hired. Even though he could have typed faster and with fewer mistakes, he delegated. Churchill realized that his time was better spent on things other than typing, such as convincing as many people as he could that a racist dictator was not to be trusted or tolerated.

"Josh, are you really equating Winston Churchill quitting typing with his subsequent role in defeating the Nazis to your quitting minor van repairs?"

Yes, yes I am. It makes me feel better.

Allow me to tell you about a few much bigger things I've quit over the years. It will make me feel better, too.

I Quit the Farm

The Christmas season is one of our family's favorite times of the year. We have an abundance of Christmas traditions. We sing. We dance. We read books. We perform Christmas pageants. We watch movies. We quote *It's a Wonderful Life*. We binge on cookies, candy, sparkling grape juice, and basically all things non-paleo, non-keto, and non-good-for-us. We make giant messes. We go to a candlelight Christmas Eve service. It's the most wonderful time of the year.

One of our favorite traditions involves grabbing hot chocolate, hopping in the van, and driving all over Amarillo gazing at Christmas lights. A couple years ago, our love of this tradition sparked an idea—one that was sure to add even more fun to our Christmas season. We decided to build a drive-through Christmas lights display. The plan sounded simple enough: (a) ask some of our favorite friends and my parents to join us in building something amazing; (b) buy some land; (c) buy a few hundred thousand Christmas lights; (d) build structures on which to display said Christmas lights; and (e) flip the light switch and smile crazy, borderline maniacal Clark Griswold smiles.

What could possibly go wrong? We bought a small, 10-acre farm and got to work. We and our friends sat in our living room, channeled our inner Griswolds, and brainstormed plans for illumination. The wives created a brilliant plan, and we set about purchasing every box of LED Christmas lights we could find. And 300,000–400,000 lights later (we totally lost count), we thought we had created something pretty special. We built gingerbread houses. We built a castle. We built a giant Texas flag. We turned a barn into Noah's ark. We built a tornado. We built several tunnels of lights to drive through. The farm was lit. Amarillo seemed to like it, too. Thousands of wonderful people took time out of their evenings to drive through our 10-acre display.

But there was a problem. Our Christmas traditions changed. Evenings were no longer spent watching movies and eating candy. Evenings were spent splicing wires, yelling at rabbits that chewed up said wires, supervising employees, and trying to avoid freezing to death. While we loved how it turned out, we had underestimated how big of an operation our drive-through light display would become. We had underestimated how much time it would take away from our families during our favorite time of the year. By the time January came, we were all exhausted. But the feedback was overwhelmingly positive, so we bought more lights, planned big improvements for the next Christmas season, and hoped that hiring more employees would lessen our workload.

By mid-December of our second year of operation, thousands more had driven through our lights display. Unfortunately, hiring more employees hadn't lessened our workload. Worse, it was becoming apparent that our big-picture plans would turn our Christmas lights extravaganza into full-time jobs for all of us for at least the next two Christmas seasons. There are times in life when reality ruins a wonderful dream. This was one of those times. If we continued making things bigger, better, and brighter each year, the farm o' lights would not be adding to or enhancing our pile of beloved family Christmas traditions; it would be replacing them for the foreseeable future. I missed singing. I missed dancing. I missed reading. I missed movies. I missed family.

I loved many things about the lights. I didn't want to quit. We'd poured enormous amounts of time, energy, and money into the idea. The potential was huge. Fortunately, my friends and my wife were the voices of reason and talked me out of stupidity. They reminded me of something very important: we'd rather our kids looked back and remembered Mom and Dad sitting around with them eating way too much chocolate and quoting cheesy lines from *White Christmas*. We'd rather our kids had those memories than the memories our kids likely had about our two years of light farm operation— Mom and Dad bolting out the door night after night uttering various discouraging words about the dang wire-chewing rabbits. Shout out to my wise wife and wise friends. Had it not been for them, I would have pushed forward and been perpetually tormented by the ghost of Christmas future.

I didn't press forward, though. I quit. We sold the farm.

I'm just as confident that we could have turned the light farm into a massive attraction as I am that I could have eventually fixed the vacuum line issue in the van. The latter would have cost me dearly in the form of countless hours, loss of my sanity, and a 71 percent chance at an emergency room visit. The former would have cost me far more. Sometimes, perseverance isn't a good thing. Sometimes life is better when you quit things.

I Quit Lowering My Kids' Expectations

If you took the time to read the introduction to this book, you may recall the story of my eldest daughter praying for a big sister and my trying to get her to quit being hopeful. Foolishly, I used to do that sort of thing quite often.

In 2014, my oldest daughter (who was 10 years old at the time) decided that she wanted to raise some money for her favorite cause—Christian Relief Fund. Much like her momma, she has a soft spot for orphans. She brainstormed ideas and eventually settled on hosting an art show with a goal of raising $500—the cost of purchasing a dairy cow for a small village in Africa. She teamed up with her sisters and some friends, and the Creative Arts Gala was born. They spent months creating all sorts of art for display and sale at the event. They created invitations and invited everyone they knew. I thought they would be lucky to raise a couple hundred dollars, and I figured most of that money would come from their generous grandparents. I tried to gently lower their expectations.

"You know, at most art shows, most of the art doesn't sell. Even great artists are sometimes lucky to sell a few paintings," I warned her.

"Don't get discouraged if you don't raise enough money to buy a cow. You're raising awareness, and that's a great thing," I encouraged her.

My daughters sold every painting and raised $2,021. They bought a dairy cow and established a feeding program that, to this day, feeds hungry orphans and widows of a small village in rural Kenya. To date, they've raised more than $14,000 through this annual Creative Arts Gala. Oh me of little faith.

"Let no one despise you for your youth, but set the believers an example in speech, in conduct, in love, in faith, in purity" (1 Tim. 4:12).

I Quit Counting to 10

Our kids are amazing. Sure, they have their share of challenging moments, many of which you've already read about. In the chapters to come, you'll read about some doozies. However, I'd put all of them up against any other kids on the planet. Generally speaking, they are well-behaved, respectful, caring, creative, and Jesus-loving kids. We're so very proud of all of them. From the time they were little, we often received compliments about how well-behaved they were in restaurants, in grocery stores, on airplanes, on buses, in church, and in other public places. God blessed us with truly wonderful kids. They are so wonderful, in fact, that we are often asked how we raised such great kids.

"By the grace of God, because we mess up a lot," I reply.

I don't want to take anything away from how hard our kids have worked to represent themselves and our family in public or how well they handle criticism and discipline in general. But one piece of parenting advice is worth noting. It's a piece of advice we were given early on that we believe played a strong role in shaping our kids' public behavior. Quit counting to 10.

Back when we had six kids under the age of six, bystanders would often marvel at their obedience in the McDonald's play area. We would yell only once into the chaos. "It's time to go! Everyone come get your shoes on!" All six kids would almost immediately file out of the play area. None of them had to be asked more than once. None of them had to be negotiated with. There were no tears.

"How'd you do that?" bystanders asked.

"Shock collars," I answered.

After taking a moment to adequately appreciate the look of horror on the faces of complete strangers, I explained that I was, of course, kidding. If they really pressed me for a legitimate answer, I sometimes passed along the advice we were given that put an end to the vast majority of the negotiating, begging, and pleading in our home and in public. Quit counting to 10.

Allow me to expound. Our kids learned from the earliest ages that there was no other option but to exit the play area when we told them to. We didn't count to 10. We didn't even count to one. We said, "It's time to leave. Everyone get your shoes on." Defiance, whining, begging, pleading, or sobbing was met with instant punishment, something like a light thump on the back of the hand along with an unemotional, calm-voiced no. "When we say it's time to go, you need to walk to your shoes and begin putting them on." That was all it took for them to get the message. In fact, it only took a couple of times, and that was the end of it.

Do you know what didn't work? "You have until the count of 10 to get out of the play area and start putting your shoes on." Do you know what a child hears when you say, "You'd better stop whining by the time I count to 10"? He or she hears, "You've got 10 more seconds of punishment-free whining. You had better make it count!"

Do you know what a child hears when they say things such as "Puhhleeeeeeaaaassssse, Momma! Just five more minutes? Please, please, please, please, please, please!" and you reply, "No. Two more minutes and then we're leaving"? They hear, "Great news! Parental directives are open to negotiation! In fact, maybe all parental directives involving leaving, parting, or otherwise stopping doing things are open to negotiation. Bedtime? Snack time? Video game time? If seven pleases bought me two more minutes, I wonder how many minutes 37 pleases will buy me."

There's a reason the United States doesn't negotiate with terrorists. There's also a reason you should quit negotiating with toddlers. Counting to 10 isn't training your kids to be well-behaved after 10 seconds. Counting to 10 is basically your kid training you that they are allowed to act like a heathen for 10 seconds before they begin (and likely control) the negotiation process. Quit counting to 10.

I Quit Thinking I Knew Everything

It was 2001. I was 21 years old when my hot girlfriend and I signed up for our first mission trip to Kenya. I prepped for the trip by reading *Celebration of Discipline* along with a healthy dose of Max Lucado and C. S. Lewis. I knew everything about everything. I wasn't sure what I was going to do during our two months there, but I figured I'd bring joy to the joyless, hope to the hopeless, and fix the entire economy of Kenya in the process. There was at least a small chance that I'd win a Nobel Prize or something. They'd probably write songs about me upon my return. I also planned to propose to my girlfriend during the trip. She'd be so amazed with my evangelical prowess and ability to singlehandedly jump-start the economy of Kenya that she'd be unable to say no. The trip was going to be legendary.

After a bit of time in Nairobi, our guide drove us far out into the bush. Our first stop was the mud hut of a new convert to Christianity. I was told he had some questions about his newfound faith. "Awesome!" I thought. My moment had come. I had prepared for this moment for a year. I was prepared to answer any question this new Christian might throw at me and quote some C. S. Lewis in the process. I introduced myself as I entered the hut and, with the help of my interpreter, made small talk for a few minutes. Finally, I asked the question (with a bit too much excitement in my voice): "So, I hear you have some questions about your faith. Can you tell me one of them?"

There was a bit of an awkward pause. I wasn't exactly sure what was coming, but I knew some God-inspired, ingenious response was going to come spilling out of my mouth. I just hoped my interpreter was up to the task of keeping up with me. Then the man spoke.

"Before I became a Christian, I married two wives. Now I'm a Christian. Which wife do I divorce?" he asked matter-of-factly.

Uh oh. Like an idiot, I stared blankly back at the man in silence. I glanced awkwardly side to side in hopes that someone would jump in with an answer. I had absolutely no response. Thanks for nothing, C. S. Lewis. Fortunately, my Kenyan guide took pity on me and answered. In case you are curious, his answer was something like this: "Don't divorce either of your wives. Treat them both as the Bible commands, and don't take any more wives." I don't remember exactly, though. I was too busy marveling at my own stupidity, theologically speaking.

I learned a number of valuable lessons that day, but here's the one I try to carry with me. Studying theology is important but not as important as taking the time to engage people. You could spend a lifetime studying theology and still not know everything. It's okay to not have all the answers. In fact, I've found that people tend to like me more when I don't have all the answers than when I act like I do. There's more room for discussion. There's more room for relationship. Oh, and there's less room for pride. Sometimes the best place to study theology isn't in a book; it's at a dinner table with people who look and think differently than you do. Or it's in a mud hut with people who barely speak your language. Sometimes it's best to quit being a know-it-all.

If I'm even slightly representative of my generation, we all need to get better at quitting things that don't matter so we can spend more time on things that do.

We need to quit putting our love of information and knowing it all over our love for knowing people.

We need to quit our phone addictions so we can build stronger real-life relationships.

We need to quit waiting until our houses are completely fixer-uppered before we invite friends and neighbors over for dinner.

We need to quit sending only "thoughts and prayers" and start sending our time, talents, and treasures.

We need to quit keyboard-warrioring against people with whom we disagree and start buying them coffee.

We need to quit striving to relive the joys of the past and start creating adventures of the future.

We need to quit prioritizing money and start prioritizing relationships.

And finally, we need to quit selfie-ing our way through life and start doing, well, pretty much anything else.

Sometimes, life is better when you quit things.

CHAPTER 8
THE CRACKED WINDSHIELD

The windshield is cracked.

While annoying, this was clearly the least of our problems. End of chapter.

CHAPTER 9
THE PRICING STRUGGLE

I looked the van up on Kelley Blue Book. $4,396. Unfortunately, Kelley Blue Book only allows me to choose between the following conditions: excellent, very good, good, and fair. I chose "fair" since "sad" was not an option. I've adjusted my asking price accordingly.

In a previous life, I provided financial marital and premarital counseling to couples. Do you know what I learned? Newlyweds and oldlyweds carry around a lot of buyer's and seller's remorse.

Buyer's remorse. When you're single, it's a fairly simple but depressing phenomenon. It usually happens when you overpay for something such as a used van you bought from a semi-humorous, viral ad on Craigslist. When you're single, buyer's remorse equals this: "I regret spending too much money on a car." In a marriage, though, buyer's remorse is more complicated. If my counseling experience was indicative of marriages as a whole, buyer's remorse in marriage involves one spouse being remorseful about the other spouse's stupid purchase. When you're married, buyer's remorse equals this: "I regret that my husband buys things an idiot would buy." Fight ensues. Teeth are gnashed. Words are growled.

Perhaps you've experienced buyer's remorse or seller's remorse in your marriage. I certainly have.

I'll get to our marital issues related to balancing buyer's and seller's remorse as well as the struggle of pricing the Struggle Bus. But first, allow me to tell you a story that will make all of us feel better. It's a story about a guy I'll call "Netflix Bob," and I'll call the story "Netflix Bob's Buyer's Remorse."

69

The last time I cleaned out my bathroom drawers—which was somewhere between five and 10 years ago (not an exaggeration), I found a couple of Walmart gift cards. Our DVD player had recently died a toddler-induced death, so the timing was perfect. I drove straight over to Walmart and purchased a fancy new Blu-ray player. It was a "smart" player that allowed me to stream Netflix, Vudu, Pandora, and more. After we put the kids to bed that night, I plopped myself down onto my bed and started setting up my new toy. I connected the player to our Wi-Fi and pushed the Netflix button to connect the player to our Netflix account.

To my surprise, Netflix popped up as if I'd already logged in. I scrolled down a bit. "Top 10 recommendations for Netflix Bob." (His name was not actually Netflix Bob, but his real name was not a terribly common name. So I'm going to call him Netflix Bob to protect his identity.)

"Well, that's weird," I thought to myself. Then I solved the mystery. Someone named Netflix Bob had previously purchased (and subsequently returned) this Blu-ray player. Netflix Bob had logged in to his accounts but had forgotten to delete his Netflix account information before he returned the player to Walmart.

Undeterred, I began the process of resetting the Blu-ray player to its factory settings so I could sync my Netflix account.

"Wait a sec," I thought.

I had a realization. I had been given the power over Netflix Bob's Netflix account. "With great power comes great responsibility," according to Benjamin Parker, or Uncle Ben of the *Spider-Man* comics.[1]

Perhaps I should send a message to Netflix Bob somehow through Netflix. Challenge accepted.

I figured Netflix Bob might find it funny if his recently watched list was full of nothing but iCarly, Bieber, and Disney films. Well, apparently Netflix Bob had kids because his recently watched list was already full of that type of stuff.

Plan B. I scrolled up to Netflix Bob's instant queue. That's when I discovered that Netflix Bob needed Jesus. Netflix Bob, God bless him, had an

---

1. "With Great Power Comes Great Responsibility," *Spider-Man*, https://spiderman-animated .fandom.com/wiki/With_great_power_comes_great_responsibility.

instant queue chocked full of less-than-child-or-any-aged-human-appropriate titles—titles I had no idea existed on Netflix or anywhere else. I thought to myself, "Perhaps I should replace these with something more wholesome, something that will encourage a bit higher standard of morality, like *Veggie Tales*."

For the next 15 minutes or so, I deleted everything on Netflix Bob's instant queue and replaced them with classics such as *Veggie Tales: Where's God When I'm Scared*, *The Passion of the Christ*, *Fireproof*, and so on.

I'm not sure what Netflix Bob thought about all this when he logged back in to his account. Perhaps he thought God was trying to speak to him through his Netflix account. Sorry, Netflix Bob. It was not the hand of God on your Netflix account. It was a punk Walmart shopper. But I hope you checked out *Veggie Tales: The Pirates Who Don't Do Anything*. There's a part at the end with a Rock Monster. Loved it. But I digress.

Don't worry, Netflix Bob. I did completely reset the Blu-ray player. Your account was deleted, and I no longer have access to it. That said, if your instant queue changes again, it might just be God trying to send you a message.

The next time you or your spouse are experiencing buyer's remorse or seller's remorse, just remember that it could be worse. You could be Netflix Bob, someone who not only had buyer's remorse but also accidentally exposed his private Netflix intrigues to our family—and now you.

When pricing the Struggle Bus, Careese and I wanted to avoid both buyer's remorse and seller's remorse. In other words, we wanted our buyer to feel as though he or she received a good deal, and we wanted to feel like we didn't rip ourselves off in the process. Unfortunately, we were facing an uphill battle. You see, when it comes to pricing things, we are a terrible combination. My wife is great at pricing things to sell, but she has been known to overpay when buying things, usually due to her strong desire to avoid haggling or her sometimes overly generous personality. On the other hand, I love haggling and am pretty good at getting a decent price when buying things. But I have been known to drastically underprice things when selling them—primarily out of a fear of accidentally ripping people off. We've had more than a few minor (and a couple not-so-minor) tiffs that resulted either from (a) my selling an old item of ours for far less than

I should have or (b) her allowing an overly nice salesperson to overcharge her for something.

What follows is the story of one of the biggest and most utterly ridiculous fights we've had in years.

My wife called me at the office and said, "Hey, the greatest thing just happened! Some people were going door to door selling frozen beef, seafood, chicken, and stuff." Then she proceeded to tell me lots of details about their lives, their families, and stuff I totally ignored because I knew where the conversation was going and didn't like it.

"Was it Schwan's?" I asked.

"No, it was some other company," she replied.

"So you don't know the name of the company?"

"Not off the top of my head," she said.

"Wait. You know their kids' names, where they go to church, and pretty much their entire family history, but you don't know the name of the company you just bought meat from? How much did it cost us?" I asked nervously.

"It was $400. But we won't have to buy meat for a couple months, and it will save me a ton of work!"

"Are they coming over for dinner?" I asked. That may seem like a crazy question to you, but for me, the question has become routine. We've played spontaneous host to a litany of random people my wife has befriended over the years—salespeople, contractors, parents of kids' friends, refugees, widows, library patrons, and so forth. My wife loves people, and she loves telling them about Jesus even more.

"Not this time," she replied.

"Let me get this straight. Traveling meat salespeople came to our door. Traveling. Meat. Salespeople. You could have said, 'No, thank you. We try not to buy our meat from random strangers driving around our neighborhood.' Instead, you spent your afternoon befriending these people and blew most of our grocery budget on their overpriced meat. So now, not only is our freezer full of meat that may or may not meet USDA standards, but a group of meat vagabonds has our address and the knowledge that the Wood family are the kind of people who buy their meat from traveling meat salespeople. How on earth is that a good thing?"

Marriage tip: when your wife starts a conversation with, "The greatest thing just happened," the wrong response is any response that blends mockery with sarcasm.

The fight was on. I'll spare you the gory details of the war and jump to the conclusion. I lost. I lost in a way that had me apologizing and acknowledging that building relationships sometimes requires overspending on food.

Yes, my wife sometimes overpays for items we buy. And yes, I struggle pricing the items we sell. I hate it. I'm afraid that I'm either (a) going to forget one of said item's deficiencies and price it too high, thus ripping off some poor, unsuspecting soul; or (b) going to let my frustrations with the item cause me to price it too low, thus ripping off myself. The end result is a pricing-bipolar personality that I'll call Garage-Sale Josh. Needless to say, hosting a garage sale is not a marriage-building experience for us. Garage-Sale Josh is one of my least favorite versions of Josh, just behind on-camera-TV Josh and just-figured-out-he's-wrong-about-something-mid-argument Josh.

Don't get me wrong. My wife and I both love going to other people's garage sales. Haggling over other people's junk is a great American pastime, and we wholeheartedly support it. However, hosting our own garage sale is terrible. First, 100 hours of pricing, setting up, cleaning, and sign-making seems like an enormous amount of time and effort to expend to profit $27. And I hate being on the haggle-ee side of the barter conversation. Haggle-er = great and fun. Love it. Haggle-ee = painful and confusing. Hate it.

Here's a semi-hypothetical scenario:

Garage sale-er: "Sir, you have a $100 price tag on this table. It seems to wobble a bit. Also, one edge appears to be covered with tiny teeth marks. Would you take less for it?"

Garage-Sale Josh: "I totally forgot about that wobble. It was, indeed, super annoying. Actually, I sort of hated that table. I'll take $4. Will that work?"

Garage sale-er: "Really?"

Garage-Sale Josh: "Wait, no. Sorry. It's still a decent table. How about $95?"

Garage sale-er: "What is happening right now? How much money do you want for the table?"

Garage-Sale Josh: "Hang on a second. Let me ask Google. This is going to take a few minutes."

Garage sale-er: "Would you take $60?"

Garage-Sale Josh (totally ignoring the question): "One time, we were eating dinner at this table, and my son was so tired that he fell asleep eating his spaghetti. He face-planted right there [points to spot on table] into a plate of saucy noodles. It was hilarious!"

Garage sale-er: "I bet that would have been funny had I been there. Again, would you take $60?"

Garage-Sale Josh: "Well, our family has had many, many wonderful memories at this table. Some of our kids took their first bites at this table. Some of our kids bit this table [points to tiny toothmarks on the table]. I don't think I can sell it for less than $500."

Garage sale-er: [rolls eyes and walks away]

You get the point. I'm a terrible price-er of things. Lord, help us if we ever decide to sell our house. I pity the unlucky real estate person who gets that job. See Chapter 14.

Now that you have a better picture of our pricing personalities, let's get back to the Struggle Bus. When the time came to put a price on the van, I knew I was in for an internal struggle. We'd sold a few cars before. Here's how the first one went down.

When we were newly married, we bought a jet-black Pontiac Firebird on eBay for approximately $5,000. It was sort of stupid and impractical, but we loved it. It had a T-top. My wife looked extra hot in that car. This fact has absolutely nothing to do with the story or the book as a whole, but I thought it was worth noting.

Soon after our first baby entered the world, we knew that the Firebird's days had come to an end. Try as we might, our car seat was not designed to fit well in a Pontiac Firebird. We had to sell it. I listed the car for sale at a reasonable Blue Book price. Within a day, our first potential buyer came to examine the car. As he was looking it over, he mentioned that the window tinting was peeling.

Let's play a game. I'll let you guess which one of the following four responses was my actual response when he pointed out the window tinting issue:

1. Like a rational human being, I kept my mouth shut and silently waited until he asked a question.

2. "Yes, I know. I'm sorry about that. It's always been that way, but I think this is a fair price."
3. "Yes, I know. However, I've only recently listed the car for sale, so I'm not willing to lower the price for at least a couple weeks for this issue."
4. "Oh, you're right. That's annoying. How about I take $500 off the price?"

The correct answer is stupid answer #4. I sold a car for almost 20 percent less than Blue Book value because the window tinting was slightly peeling. Seller's remorse.

Back to pricing the van. We were facing an uphill battle, and I knew it. In the span of two minutes, my mind drifted from "I'm 90 percent sure we won't even be able to give this thing away" to "These vans are hard to find and seem to be selling for a ton more than their book value on Cars.com. I guess we should try to get more money out of it."

Ultimately, we turned to Kelley Blue Book and NADA.

My wife looked up the Kelley Blue Book value and laughed.

"What are you laughing at?" I asked.

"This site's valuation tool only gives me the options of good and fair." She snickered.

I immediately knew why she was laughing. We both spent the next 30 minutes or so reminiscing and laughing about all the reasons "fair" was a generous description at best for the Struggle Bus. The ad was born.

It is worth noting that I also looked up NADA value. Because I think that you, the reader, would like to laugh along with me, allow me to present to you the NADA clean retail value—[drumroll] $7,900. The only way this van of ours was worth $7,900 was if the speaker hole had been stuffed with hundred-dollar bills. Spoiler alert: it had not. NADA value was useless to me.

You've read the ad. Over the course of nine years, our family of 11 slowly, methodically, and aromatically gave our 2005 Ford van a beatdown for the ages. The Struggle Bus had lived a hard knock life. I still wasn't exactly sure what price to list the van, but we decided there was going to be little risk of accidentally underpricing it.

Ultimately, we decided to take $500 off the Kelley Blue Book price and hope for the best. It seemed okay to me to price it at $3,800. We figured we could always lower the price in a couple weeks if we didn't have any offers. Within 48 hours, we had multiple offers from all over the country.

In hindsight, I suppose we should have priced it higher.

Wait, no. Any vehicle that has ever been referred to as a "rolling dumpster" should not be valued at more than $3,800.

Wait, no. As was suggested to me by a number of folks, I should have bumped up the price after it went viral. We could have used the extra money to buy a plethora of Chick-fil-A nuggets to replace all the ones lost to the speaker hole.

Wait, no. That's stupid. The van went viral because of its lack of value. The new owners definitely overpaid. I feel guilty.

Wait, no. The new owners had the van checked out by a professional. It's bound to be worth more than what they paid. I feel great about that.

Ugh. I have issues. I shouldn't be allowed to price things.

Wait. Oh no! I've become Netflix Bob! Netflix Bob didn't clean out his Netflix history. I didn't clean out the speaker hole. Netflix Bob left a slew of tawdry titles on his Netflix queue. We could have easily left baby teeth or slime or Band-Aids or rotten fruit or God only knows what else in addition to old chicken nuggets.

The moral of the story: Don't be me or Netflix Bob. Of course, we should all try not to be disgusting in the first place, but in the event your messiness has exploded into a speaker hole or onto your Netflix account, clean that stuff out, especially before you sell anything containing it. You'll save yourself some seller's remorse.

Aside from the realization that I've become Netflix Bob, we're happy we sold the van at what we think was a fair price. I hope the new owners find it well worth their money, make tons of new memories, and find a few dollars amid the depravity of the speaker hole.

CHAPTER 10
THE STUFF THAT ACTUALLY WORKS

The heater works. Also, the van has a hitch and wiring for a trailer.

Those two sentences are boring. The best stories in life don't usually come when things work as they are supposed to. The best stories usually come when things don't go as planned. That said, I've decided that this chapter will not be devoted to fully functioning, boring heater and trailer parts. This chapter will instead be devoted to the story of a road trip that didn't work out as planned. I know, I know. A random road trip story doesn't fit the theme of the book so far. I've given it some thought and have decided I don't care. That's the luxury of writing a book. I can write what I want. Here's the story of a road trip—a road trip that shows that sometimes, even when the van worked, other things didn't.

Traveling is one of our favorite things to do as a family. We love to see things. We love to meet new people. We love to cram our whole family into the van, get out on the open road, sing some songs, and force our kids to bond and love one another. Sure, there are moments of "What on earth were we thinking?" There are moments where "Dad-speak" inadvertently and uncontrollably shoots out of my mouth. "WE'LL BE THERE WHEN WE GET THERE!" "I'LL PULL THIS VAN OVER!" "IF YOU GUYS CAN'T DECIDE ON A MOVIE, I'M PICKING THE MOVIE, AND YOU'RE ALL GOING TO HAVE TO WATCH *THE WIGGLES* AGAIN!" For the most part, though, my wife and kids are the best travelers on the planet.

Several years back, we decided to take a summer road trip to San Diego, which is more than 1,000 miles from Amarillo, so we knew the trip would be epic. We had planned a few adventures for our time there, but the highlight would be the Big Bay Boom July 4 fireworks show. (Side note: July 4 is one of our favorite days of the year. We usually spend the day celebrating all things America and freedom and amber waves of grain. We go to the local parade. We listen to patriotic music. We prepare and consume red, white, and blue food. We wear red, white, and blue clothes. We generally live out the day in ways that would make bald eagles weep tears of joy. Coincidentally, my wife's 2017 July 4 shirt had a picture on it of a bald eagle shedding a patriotic tear.) Anyhow, when we heard that San Diego had one of the largest and best fireworks displays in the country, we couldn't resist. Our plan was to drive as far as we could make it each day. We would stop when we got tired but make sure we made it to San Diego for July 4. We booked no hotels ahead of time except for a couple nights in San Diego. Sure, it's an awfully risky travel game to play with a big family, but we learned something early on in our married life. You can devote all your extra time and energy to planning every detail of a vacation, but it often doesn't matter. Things never go according to plan. Fortunately, as I've already mentioned, the best memories often come when things don't go according to plan. Call it whimsical. Call it stupid. Whatever. We have a great time, and playing the hotel lottery has only failed us once or twice.

We loaded up the Struggle Bus with all the things a large family is required to take on a road trip—strollers, diapers, Pack 'n Play, Cheerios, clothes, blankets, pacifiers, Tylenol, beef jerky, towels, travel pillows, DVDs, CDs, headphones, sippy cups, melatonin (which I promise was not in the sippy cups), iPad, iPods, water bottles, somewhere between 80 and 100 various charger cables, wet wipes, empty grocery bags, Pepto Bismol, jumper cables, playing cards, Band-Aids, Dr. Pepper, amoxicillin, and, since there was still a tiny bit of space remaining, the children. Needless to say, the back end of the van was transformed into a veritable cornucopia of kid junk. My accidental purchase of a 15-passenger van instead of a 12-passenger van was paying off. I applauded myself accordingly. Then off to San Diego we went.

We spent a couple days in Albuquerque. We ate at a place called the Little Red Hamburger Hut. It was a delightful little establishment, except for the restroom. It was clean; that wasn't the problem. The problem was the décor.

One of my kids exited the restroom and said (loud enough for the rest of the restaurant to hear), "Daddy, there's a sign in there that says 'If you took a @#$!, please put it back.' What does @#$! mean, and why would we take it?"

I would just as soon not had that conversation in public. Oh well. After we said our good-byes to Albuquerque, we headed to Arizona. We took some obligatory photos with giant cacti. We stood on the corner in Winslow, Arizona. It would have been such a fine sight to see, but my kids neither understood the importance of nor appreciated our singing about said corner.

After Winslow, it was time for our biggest gamble of the trip: a slight detour to Oatman, Arizona. While researching the trip, my wife had discovered this little ghost town. (She's the queen of finding fun, out-of-the-ordinary adventures.) Oatman was just about an hour off our route and a bit off the beaten path. And by "a bit," I mean it lies in the middle of nowhere in the middle of the desert. You had better make sure you have plenty of gas, water, supplies, faith, and willpower before you exit I-40 and head to Oatman. There's a scene in the movie *The Emperor's New Groove* where two of the characters, Pacha and Kuzco, are tied to a tree branch in a river and floating toward the edge of a waterfall. Pacha is facing the waterfall. Kuzco is facing the other direction and can't see the peril behind him.

Pacha: "Uh-oh."
Kuzco: "Don't tell me. We're about to go over a huge waterfall."
Pacha: "Yep."
Kuzco: "Sharp rocks at the bottom?"
Pacha: "Most likely."
Kuzco: "Bring it on."

That's a bit how we felt as I-40 drifted farther and farther into the rear view.

"Nothing but sweltering desert and misery around us if the van breaks down or we get lost?"

"Most likely."

"Bring it on."

Fortunately, the van powered through the narrow, winding, and seemingly endless desert roads. We arrived safely in Oatman. The first thing we noticed were the donkeys that were everywhere. At the time, we had seven kids—seven kids in a town of wild donkeys. They thought Oatman was the greatest thing ever. We might as well have been at Disney World. As you might imagine, though, the donkeys were not as excited about our kids as our kids were about them. So we gave the donkeys a break from kid ambush and slipped into a restaurant-bar for lunch. For me, entering the restaurant was a bit like entering Narnia. The entire place was covered in dollar bills. Stapled to the walls. Hanging from the ceiling. Taped to the bar. Dollars everywhere. There must have been a hundred thousand dollars in the place. It looked how I would imagine Jay-Z's living room to look. I don't remember if the food was good or not, but who cares? THE ENTIRE RESTAURANT AND BAR WERE COVERED IN DOLLAR BILLS. How cool is that? After I begrudgingly left the restaurant, we explored the rest of Oatman, including a motorcycle museum that housed a few really old Harley Davidsons. I know less about motorcycles than I do about vans, but I thought they were super awesome and posted a photo of them on Instagram so my followers would think I was cooler than I am.

We spent longer in Oatman than originally planned and then headed out for our ultimate destination: San Diego. See you later, Oatman. We'll be back, and hopefully this ridiculous book will send a few more tourists your way. You earned it.

We arrived in San Diego a couple days before the Fourth of July. As soon as we arrived, Careese started researching various adequately star-spangled entertainment options. She found a little area of town called Old Town that had converted the town square into a colonial-themed July 4 party. It sounded awesome, so off we went. It did not disappoint. It felt as though the entire citizenry of the town donned colonial-themed costumes. There were cake walks, square dances, stagecoach rides, face paintings, Declaration of Independence signings, and potato sack races. A Benjamin Franklin look-a-like even read the Declaration of Independence from a star-spangled-bunting-lined stage. God bless America. George Washington would have been proud of us all. Real proud.

After several hours of glorious American revelry, we headed out to San Diego Bay to ready ourselves for the fireworks show of a lifetime. We were told there would be more than 200,000 people in attendance, so we arrived several hours early to stake out a prime spot on the lawn by the shore. After a bit of roaming in the lovely San Diego weather, we found the spot we were looking for. It was perfect. We laid out our blankets along with an assortment of kid paraphernalia that had been smuggled out of the van. We spent the next few hours playing tag, duck-duck-goose, and more. That is one of the joys of having a big family. There's built-in entertainment. You can play games that other families can't. Well, I suppose a small family can play duck-duck goose, heads up 7-up, freeze tag, and such, but the games would probably be much shorter.

At last, the sky grew dark, and the growing horde of humanity began to settle down in anticipation of the coming show. The fireworks were set to go off from four barges just offshore. At last, it was time, and 200,000 of our closest friends grew silent as the show began. Four giant, balloon-shaped balls of light emerged from each barge. They remained lit for about 15 seconds. It was certainly different than any other fireworks show intro I had ever seen, but it was awesome. We and everyone else cheered what we all thought was the greatest fireworks intro of all time. Then there was silence. Nothing happened. No fireworks. Only silence. After a few minutes had passed, the crowd began to mumble. Still nothing. Slowly, the crowd's mumble started to light up with the shimmer of thousands of phone screens. Everyone was searching for the reason for the delay. Unfortunately, the mass of humanity had destroyed cell service in the area. No one could connect to the outside world. The crowd was forced to talk to each other like it was 1776. Still, no one could figure out what was happening.

My hometown of Amarillo happens to be known as one of the windiest cities in America. We are used to fireworks shows being delayed by wind or weather, but the weather in San Diego was perfect. The sky was clear. The weather couldn't have been the problem. Thirty minutes went by. Still nothing. Finally, after almost 45 minutes, someone in the crowd heard the cause of the problem on one of the local radio stations (note to any kids reading this: radio was a thing that was kind of like Spotify, Apple Music, or Pandora, but you can't pause it, and someone else chooses the playlist for everyone.) Person by person, the news finally made its way to our section of the grass.

A technical malfunction had caused all the fireworks to go off at once. Those balls of light we saw were the product of every single firework being ignited at the same time. That was it. The show was over. Hours of waiting culminated in a 15-second ball of flames. In case you, like me, have always wondered what it would look like if every firework purchased for a fireworks show ignited at once, here's your answer. It forms a pretty spectacular (albeit short-lived) blaze of glory, but it's more smoky than sparkly.

The time had come to relay the news to our children. Unfortunately, I had set myself up for disaster. You see, there's an ill-advised and risky trick you learn as a parent when you find yourself in a situation where you need your kids to wait patiently. It's called hype. Here's how it works. Suppose you're waiting for a movie to start and your children are getting restless. You see a certain look in their eyes. It's the same look Bruce Banner gets before he transforms into the Incredible Hulk. What do you say?

"Just hang in there for a few more minutes. This movie is going to be worth it. You're going to love it! Let me tell you what I'm most excited about. What are you most excited about?"

Then, you proceed to have a conversation about the mind-blowing greatness that is about to befall your children. This tactic can work pretty well to keep children excited while simultaneously preventing them from turning into a loud, angry mob of fit-throwing, Incredible Hulk-ish, cry-sack monsters. I'm speaking hypothetically, of course.

Unfortunately, hype can backfire. Specifically, hype can backfire when the event you've been hyping explodes into a literal ball of flames. The greater the disappointment, the more energy for the little Hulks.

We broke the news to our kids. The event I may or may not have billed as "the greatest fireworks show of all time" was not going to happen. Our kids would not be seeing "more fireworks in the sky than you can imagine." Instead, our kids would be seeing the inside of the van for however many hours it took to drive through the hundred thousand people's worth of traffic that stood between us and our hotel. I braced myself for mutiny, but it didn't come. The kids were, of course, disappointed. But they chose instead to reflect on the day. We had played games. We had eaten an abundance of patriotic snacks. We had witnessed the simultaneous explosion of hundreds of fireworks, and no one had died—us included. All in all, it had been a truly wonderful day. The kids laughed and reminisced on the drive back to the hotel until, one by one, they all fell asleep.

That's when I realized that my kids had a greater tolerance for disappointment than I did. Parenting can often be humbling like that. As it turned out, my kids weren't the ones who needed the hype. I was. Our entire trip had been planned around one destination—one event that had turned out to be a bust. I had been so focused on the hyped destination that I had expected its failure to ruin the whole journey. Fortunately, my kids reminded me of a lesson we all learn in Life 101. It's often important to shift focus away from the hype of the destination and toward the joys of the journey.

That's the story of our trip to San Diego in a nutshell, but it's also the story of our van. A trip can culminate in an event that lets you down, but the journey can still be better than you could have ever imagined. A van's life can end in a brutal Craigslist ad that lists its depravity in brutal detail, but the journey in said van can still be better than you could have ever imagined.

CHAPTER 11
THE OIL CHANGES

Q: *"Have you performed all proper maintenance*
and religiously changed the oil every 3,000 miles?"

A: *[laughter] No. No, I have not. Does this article make you feel better?*
It made me feel better: "The 3,000-Mile Oil Change
Is Pretty Much History" by Alina Tugend.

Prior to 2009 and before the Struggle Bus, we owned a Toyota Sequoia. We changed the oil every 3,000 miles. We washed it. We vacuumed it. We made the quintessential parenting rule of "no food or drinks in the Sequoia." We loved that Sequoia, but life was different then. We had two kids and one on the way. We had time for things like regular car maintenance, policing no-food-or-drink rules, and maintaining a socially acceptable level of cleanliness. Then, over the course of the next 20 months, babies three, four, five, and six came along. So long, regular maintenance. So long, no-food-or-drink rule. So long, cleanliness. So long, beloved Sequoia. Hello, Struggle Bus.

As it turns out, the progression of vehicle maintenance was, in some ways, similar to the progression of parenting a growing family. We started out as an SUV-driving, 2.3 kid-having, Jesus-loving, middle-class American stereotype. Then gradually, but seemingly overnight, we were no longer a stereotype. Jesus was just about the only common denominator between our old life and new, but even our religion changed a bit as Jesus became more necessity than accessory.

When you become a parent, you realize you are capable of feeling an overwhelming sense of inadequacy, love, gratefulness, excitement, fear, happiness, worry, joy, and exhaustion—all at the same time. The increase in the size of our family brought with it a simultaneous increase in the intensity of each of those feelings. Personally, as a parent of a large family (and this is my totally unscientific theory), I think prolonged exposure to such extreme feelings of inadequacy, love, exhaustion, and such has made me a bit overly calloused at times to the world around me. I think that is part of the reason things like regular oil changes aren't as high on my priority list as they used to be. If you're a parent of a large family, perhaps you've felt a similar progression.

Family vehicle #1: "Oh no! The service engine light came on! Let's go straight to the mechanic and get it checked out."

Family vehicle #2: "I've tried resetting it twice, and the service engine light is still on. It's been a week, so I guess I should find time to take it to the mechanic."

Family vehicle #2 after kid #8: "But is there smoke?"

. . .

Kid #1: "Oh no! You slightly scraped your knee. You have a tiny scratch and you're almost bleeding? Yes, of course I'll get you seven Band-Aids and a bag of ice. Sure, we can snuggle and read *Wacky Wednesday* for the bajillionth time!"

Kid #2: "I'm sorry you slightly scraped your knee. Did you get blood on anything? You know where the Band-Aids are."

Kid #8: "But did you die?"

. . .

Family vehicle #1: "No. You know the rule. Don't even ask. You cannot bring your food into the car."

Family vehicle #2: "Yes, you can eat your lunch in the car. Please try not to make a mess."

Family vehicle #2 after kid #8: "Your lunch from yesterday is still in the car. Just eat that."

. . .

Kid #1: "Is your bed made, hair brushed, and teeth brushed? If so, go get dressed. Your clothes are laid out on your bed for you."

Kid #2: "Those clothes don't match. Please change into some clothes that match. Did you remember to brush your teeth?"

Kid #8: "Spider-Man mask, Sheriff Woody shirt, pajama shorts, and cowboy boots. Huh? That's a bold fashion choice, son, but please get in the car. We're 20 minutes late to everywhere."

. . .

Family vehicle #1: "It's been 2,998 miles since our last oil change, and we're two miles from the oil change shop. I'll drive over right now and get it changed with synthetic oil, and I'll replace the air filter while I'm at it."

Family vehicle #2: (Remembering it has been almost 4,000 miles since the last oil change, I drive to the oil change shop.) "It's $59 for an oil change? Forget that!" (I procrastinate for almost another 1,000 miles and then return.) "Fine. Change my oil, but just bang the air filter on the ground until it looks clean-ish. I'm not paying to replace it."

Family vehicle #2 after kid #8: "I don't remember if I changed my oil last week or last decade. Is there such a thing as Great Value brand oil?"

. . .

Kid #1: "That's the most beautiful picture of a turkey anyone has ever drawn! Yes, of course we'll display it on our refrigerator and subsequently keep it forever!"

Kid #2: "That is a wonderful drawing of a turkey! Let me take a picture of it before you put it on the refrigerator in case it gets lost or accidentally thrown in the trash."

Kid #8: "I just found your wonderful drawing of a turkey. It was crammed in the speaker hole along with your chicken nuggets."

. . .

You know what it's like having a fourth kid? Imagine you're drowning, then someone hands you a baby.[1]

—Jim Gaffigan

When you have a large family such as ours, you attract a fair amount of attention wherever you go. That may sound weird to those with normal-sized families, but inquisitions by complete strangers are commonplace in our life.

---

1. Drew Wood, "12 Jim Gaffigan Quotes & Jokes: Everything You Need to Know about Family & Parenting," *Fatherly*, https://www.fatherly.com/love-money/relationships/everything-you-need-to-know-about-parenting-in-12-jim-gaffigan-quotes/.

We field a steady barrage of questions wherever we go. Yesterday, a nice lady we'd never met asked us how long we'd been married, where we lived, and how much money we spent each month on housing. We've learned to embrace this phenomenon as an opportunity to meet new people and maybe tell them a bit about Jesus. We've shared coffee and meals with a number of these strangers over the years. Yes, we're crazy like that. In the course of these conversations, we are often asked questions about how we manage life with all the kids along with the usual queries: Are you Mormon or Catholic? Do you know what causes that? How do you survive? I could summarize our answer to the survival and life management questions as follows: preventative maintenance.

As your family grows and your world gets busier, it becomes harder and harder to make time for preventative maintenance on anything—cars, kids, friends, house, marriage, anything. Ironically, though, the more chaotic life gets, the more important preventative maintenance becomes. Changing the oil every 3,000 to 5,000 miles may not be ideal, but at least it keeps the car going. Never changing your oil, though, is bad. Very bad. The car stops moving. It dies. It catches on fire. Neglecting your marriage or kids or house or friendships can have equally bad consequences. The relationships can stop moving forward. They can die. In the midst of our chaotic world, we've discovered several practical preventative maintenance things that keep our family chugging along.

Before I dole out advice, I need to add this preface because I don't want you to get the wrong idea. Most days, I don't feel like I'm in the position to be doling out advice. I practice what I preach a lot like I practice oil changes on the van. Sometimes I'm right on time. Other times, I'm a couple thousand miles past the due date. Sometimes I put in the minimum required oil with a bad attitude. Sometimes I merrily use synthetic oil. I'm erratic and imperfect. Fortunately, I've discovered that one of the keys to living (and enjoying) life in a large family is this: imperfectly trying over and over again is better than inertia. You can't let a fear of being imperfect or of reliving a previous failure rob you or your family of the joys of action. I believe God honors our imperfect attempts more than our perfect procrastination.

Question #1: How do you build individual relationships with your kids when there are so many of them, and how do you balance that with quality family time?

Soccer. Tennis. Golf. Ballet. Piano. Guitar. Theater. Football. Youth group. Tutoring. Speech therapy. Vision therapy. That's a list of our kids' activities this fall alone. Obviously, we place value on each of these activities; otherwise, we wouldn't be involved in them. However, it can often be challenging to carve out quality family time (let alone quality one-on-one kid time) from a schedule that is monopolized by activity-to-activity mom-taxiing. I should note that one of the reasons we homeschool is so we can fit many of these activities into daytime hours rather than evening hours. That helps tremendously, of course, but our time is still pressed. As we talk to friends and complete strangers, we realize we are not alone, and not just because we have a large family. Whether you have one child or a borderline reality show-ish number of children like we do, family schedules these days can require high-level calculus to coordinate. It's no wonder American parents spend such ridiculous amounts of money each year on car payments. They spend most of their time in them. That said, we've incorporated a few habits into our day-to-day and year-to-year life that have helped us build what we feel like are pretty great relationships with our kids.

1. *Vacation.* Thanks to the viral van post that spawned this book, the world now knows that we don't spend our money on fancy cars. We do, however, spend it on vacations. As you've already gathered from the previous 10 chapters of this book, we love to travel—and not just for adventure's sake. We love to travel because it pulls our family out of the day-to-day busyness into forced family-bonding time. It gives us time to work through issues. If any of the kids are struggling to get along, we have time to lead them to solutions. Often it comes naturally to have fun together. Other times, we have to learn how to have fun together. Vacations allow time to learn these things. And we do. Also, as nerdy as it is, I try to prepare a list of questions to ask my kids over the course of our trip. These questions range from "What is your favorite thing we do as a family and why?" to "What is something you failed at this month?" to "Is _____ still your favorite food?" Of course, it isn't healthy to reduce parent-kid relationships to a formulaic, Q&A approach.

The key is intentionality. Vacation is not a time for us to retreat into an antisocial cocoon of screen time. It's a time to draw conversation out of the digital world and into reality. It's a time to draw conversation out of inner struggles and reclusiveness. Sure, conversation is sometimes a struggle. But I've found that spending a bit of time beforehand crafting a list of questions helps tremendously.

You may be thinking this is all well and good, but it doesn't answer the question of how we build individual relationships with our kids. Yes, vacation time is usually spent as a group, but here's the deal. Whether it's at mealtimes or in a car or on a plane or on a train, vacation allows abundant time for one-on-one conversations—conversations that won't be interrupted by homework or phone calls.

2. *One-on-one time.* Spending time individually with each of our kids is challenging for every reason you might imagine, but it is important. We've learned that the easiest solution is to take one kid along as we run errands. For example, we end up at the grocery store almost daily. While we try to make the trips as quickly as possible, these are great opportunities to have one-on-one time with a son or daughter. No, we don't usually buy them anything special at the store. It's just a routine trip. The goal is conversation, not candy or ice cream or a prize. Side note: This is probably a subject for another book entirely, written by someone more qualified than I am, but I think one of the most dangerous things modern society does to kids is teach them that it isn't quality time unless there's an opportunity for a social media post. Of course, neither social media posts nor candy nor prizes nor ice cream are bad in and of themselves. In fact, ice cream is proof God loves us and wants us to be happy. But they shouldn't be the backbone of the relationships you have with your kids. When it comes to parenting, presence trumps presents every time. Yes, take your kids on grand adventures, but take them on boring ones, too. They need to know that we value them more than the social media likes they give us. I don't want my kids to live life in a "pics or it didn't happen" relationship with me. Most of my best conversations with my kids haven't made the jump to social media.

I used to be baffled by how Jesus handled the people he healed. "Don't tell anyone about this" (paraphrased) seemed to be his common refrain. This struck me as odd for a guy who gave his followers the seemingly opposite message of go and tell the world about me. However, I think I get it now. Jesus wouldn't have posted every miracle on social media or uploaded selfies with the blind man with a caption or the emoticon eyes, praise hands, and 100 emojis. He wanted the individuals he healed to be absolutely clear on one thing: he healed them because he cared about them, individually. It's almost as if he were saying, "Don't tag my 'Jesus Saves' page on Facebook. I need you to know that this is about you and me, not about likes and praise hand emojis." I want my kids to get the same message from me.

3. *Songs and prayers.* In Chapter 2, I mentioned our nightly song time. We've dubbed our bedtime routine "songs and prayers." We ask the kids what we should be praying for. We take turns each night. From youngest to oldest, each kid takes a night to choose the songs we sing and to pray for our family and our collective prayer requests. Admittedly, sometimes this time is rushed. Some nights we skip song time out of exhaustion or busyness, but it has turned into one of the most important routines we have as a family. In addition to the benefits I mentioned in Chapter 2, this time has turned into a pretty solid accountability mechanism. On the nights I struggle to think of many things to pray for, it's a reminder that I'm too disconnected from the needs of the people around me. It's also a reminder that prayer is often supposed to be active. Kids are smart. If we pray for someone who is starving to death, our kids are going to ask what we are doing to help. We don't want to teach our kids to solely send thoughts and prayers. We want to teach our kids, whenever possible, to inject action into their prayers. By giving money. By giving time. By building relationships. To my knowledge, the Bible never tells us to pray for orphans and widows. It tells us to act—to defend them (Ps. 82:3) and to look after them (James 1:27). Of course, that doesn't negate the importance of praying for them, but it does emphasize the importance of action. Our family prayer time is a constant reminder for us to act—to reach out to people. It's a reminder that to really pray for people, we must take time to get to know them on a deeper level. I don't like the discomfort I feel when staring at a living room full of my kids and admitting to them that I don't have specific prayer requests. Admitting I don't have any specific prayer requests is the same as admitting I haven't taken the time to get to know anyone well enough to know their struggles or that I've taken no action to help anyone we've been praying for. While I loathe the accompanying self-guilt, it's an important accountability mechanism in my life.

Yes, it's a blessing to sing together as a family. Yes, it's a blessing to hear your kids pray. Yes, it's a time that allows us to hit the Pause button on a busy life and refocus our family. But just as important, it's a time as a family to make sure we aren't disconnecting ourselves from the world around us. It's a time to remind ourselves and our kids that we're supposed to engage the world around us actively—not passively—through prayer.

Question #2: You're a large, homeschooling family. Don't you worry about your kids growing up in an overprotective bubble?

Yes, we do worry about our kids growing up in a bubble. Having a large family can be isolating. Believe it or not, it isn't the homeschooling thing that leads to isolation. It's the friend dynamic. First, whether your family is large or small, it can be terribly intimidating to invite a large family over to your home to join you for dinner. How much should we cook? Do we have enough chairs? Are their kids going to destroy our house? Will we be able to carry on a conversation? Do we have enough toilet paper?

These are all valid questions, and they all serve as barriers to building friendships. To put it another way, suppose it is 9:00 a.m. and your plans for the evening are unexpectedly cancelled, leaving you with a free evening. Further suppose that you, for some un-twenty-first-century reason, opt for human interaction rather than binge-watching Netflix. You make an impromptu decision to invite someone over to join you for dinner. Do you invite John, Suzy, and their three-month-old Sam? Or do you invite Jim, Jane, Jim Jr., Allison, James, Caleb, Noah, Sadie, and Jessica? It's a no-brainer, right? You may love Jim and Jane. You may love their offspring. But unless you happen to have five pounds of spaghetti or a fully cooked turkey in your pantry, you'll invite John and Suzy. It's harder to invite a large family over for dinner.

Speaking on behalf of large families everywhere, not only is it challenging for friends to invite your family over for dinner, but it can be intimidating for us to host social functions or invite friends over to our home. Why? For one, large family houses are rarely completely clean. Not long after we added our seventh kid to our family, we hosted a get-together for our church small group. One of our friends started to get up from our table only to discover that both her hair and the back of her shirt were glued to our dining room chair by a healthy amount of strawberry jelly. Stuff like that is a bit embarrassing. Side note: If you want to have some fun at a gathering hosted by a large family, pretend you are going to lift up one of the couch cushions for some reason. I looked under our couch cushions a couple weeks ago. Want to know what treasures I found? Six pencils, three pens, a spoon, assorted Legos, a rock, a necklace, earrings, measuring tape, a golf tee, a quarter, a battery, a couple of fake doubloons, a peanut, some dental floss, a hair clip, a magnetic letter O, a bracelet, a couple of toys, a half-inch crescent wrench, and a goldfish cracker. One time, I found a corn dog with one bite out of it. Anyhow, inviting people over can be intimidating.

So how do we remedy these issues? For starters, we stopped caring so much. We started inviting people over when we had time, regardless of whether our house had been cleaned that day (or week) (or month). Then a funny thing happened. Our guests relaxed. They invited us over to their houses without worrying as much about presenting an image of HGTV perfection. We made all the best kinds of friends—the ones who embraced our messiness and who weren't afraid to expose a bit of their own.

If our experience is any indication, Americans' houses are only spotlessly clean on social media. We're all a little messy. We just don't want to admit it, so we don't invite people over. But messy people need community just like messy cars need regular maintenance. Here is our advice. Stop caring so much about having the perfectly clean, fixer-upper-ed house before inviting people over. People need friends more than they need spotlessness, and strawberry jelly washes out of hair easier than you might think. And keep five pounds of spaghetti in your pantry at all times.

Popping the Bubble

I think one of the most dangerous things Christians do to their kids is raise them in an isolated, socioeconomic, racial, and ideological bubble. Unfortunately, it can be easy to fall into a routine that keeps you within a tiny distance from your home, a tiny shade of color from your race, a tiny percentage of income from your level of income, and a tiny ideological distance from your theological or political ideals. "Train up a child in the way he should go; even when he is old he will not depart from it" (Prov. 22:6) is our anthem. Unfortunately, we often live our lives in more of a "Train up a child in the bubble he should be in; even when he is old he will stay in it" type of way. That said, here are a couple of habits we've formed in our attempts to pop the proverbial bubble.

Our city is home to one of the largest populations of refugees per capita in the United States. Thanks to a local organization that provides services to our city's refugee population, we've been able to connect with a number of resettled families. We try to have at least one such family over to our home for dinner fairly regularly. Their stories are fascinating. I'll never forget the first time a refugee family accepted our dinner invitation. My wife, our two oldest kids, and I sat enthralled for at least an hour as our new friends told their story. Although the details were lost a bit in translation, we understood the general story. Their Ethiopian family had fled a war-torn area to find their way to a Kenyan refugee camp and eventually boarded a plane bound for Amarillo, Texas. They endured fear, hunger, confusion, loss, exhaustion, and poverty. At one point in the story, we all sat listening with eyes and jaws wide open as one of the daughters recounted a time when she had been locked in a shipping container for days by some bad people. She was 12.

"Were you given food and water?" we asked.

"Yes, a little, but I tried not to eat or drink. They only opened the door once per day to let me outside for a short bathroom break."

Needless to say, we had virtually nothing in common with our new friends. Not nationality. Not race. Not religion. Not upbringing. Not clothing. Not income. Not education. Not profession. Not job opportunities. Not housing. Not food preference. Barely language. If you're ever struggling to find a way to expand your kids' bubble, invite a refugee family over for dinner. Connect with them by contacting the nearest refugee resettlement office and asking how to get involved. You can search your state here: https://www.acf.hhs.gov/orr/state-programs-annual-overview.

Do you sometimes find yourself struggling to come up with topics for conversation with your kids? After a meal with a refugee family, you won't lack any conversation starters on religion or race or gender or poverty or privilege or politics or life. Yes, the language barrier is uncomfortable. Yes, conversation can be difficult when you have little to relate to. Ask to hear their story. Ask what they like most about America. Ask what aspects of life in America they find to be the most challenging. You'll probably wish you had recorded their answers. I wish I had.

Another way to exit your metaphorical bubble is to travel as a family. I've already mentioned our affinity for vacations.

> Travel is fatal to prejudice, bigotry, and narrow-mindedness, and many of our people need it sorely on these accounts. Broad, wholesome, charitable views of men and things cannot be acquired by vegetating in one little corner of the earth all one's lifetime.[2]
>
> —Mark Twain

Travel makes the world come alive. Travel makes history come alive. Our kids learned about the Revolutionary War in their history books, but they grasped the story better as we stood atop Bunker Hill and had them imagine the battle that was once lost there—and the subsequent war that was won thanks in part to the battle that was lost there. We've tried to teach our kids how lucky they are to have been born in Amarillo, Texas, but they understood the abundance of their privilege much more profoundly when they held the hands of starving children in Africa and as they shared tea and bread with them in huts. We've tried to teach our kids about injustice, but they felt the weight of it much more heavily as we walked them through old Southern plantations once run on the backs of slaves. We've tried to teach our kids about evil, but its reality became much more evident as we walked in silence through the 9/11 museum. We've tried to teach our kids the contrast between living faith and dead religion, but they had a deeper understanding as we walked through monumental old buildings—buildings that once served as church buildings kept alive by communities of friends, tithes, and prayer but now serve as ornate tourist traps kept dead by the ticket fees and donations of strangers. We've tried to teach our kids to empathize with cultural outsiders, but they empathize much more when we walk the streets of a land where they are the cultural outsiders.

Travel is a wonderful teacher. And now that I have the benefit of hindsight, I've realized one more value that travel has brought to our family. It's given our kids a front-row seat to witness their parents' failures. We've missed turns. We've forgotten luggage. We've fished an exploded diaper out

2. "Mark Twain Quotes," *Goodreads*, https://www.goodreads.com/quotes/1716-travel-is-fatal-to-prejudice-bigotry-and-narrow-mindedness-and-many.

of a hotel pool. We've argued. We've yelled. We've said, "I'll pull this car over right now!" We've missed meals. We've whined. We've received a ticket for speeding. We've hit concrete barriers. We've spilled drinks. We've vomited. We've overslept. We've underslept. We've broken things. We've bragged. We've underbudgeted and stayed in some questionable motels. We've tripped and fallen. One time, we left for a month-long trip to Kenya, and I forgot to pack pants.

I think it's important for our kids to see us fail. It's important for them to see us pick ourselves up, dust ourselves off, and try again. It's important for them to hear us admit mistakes and ask for forgiveness. It's important for them to learn not to take life too seriously sometimes. Most importantly, it's important for them to learn that things don't always have to go according to plan for life to be fun. In fact, life is often the most fun when plans go completely awry. That's when adventure happens.

Our advice to you is that regular maintenance is important. Without it, something is bound to catch on fire—literally or figuratively. Get out there. Travel. Introduce your family to new people. Build relationships. Make new friends. Make mistakes. Fail. Ask forgiveness. Pick yourself up, dust yourself off, and try again.

CHAPTER 12
THE EXOTIC, OFF-ROAD ADVENTURES

Q: *"Are those 143,000 miles mostly highway miles?"*

A: Well, a lot of them are. However, we've been using this van as our farm van for the past year or so. Also, in efforts to find quicker routes, I've been known to disobey Siri's directions. These "shortcuts" have sometimes taken us on exotic, off-road adventures. I'm pretty sure those miles cancel out all of the so-called "highway miles."

Have you ever searched for a used vehicle online? As you are aware, I have. It's an exhausting process. After a couple hours of browsing, a number of common advertising phrases begin to annoy me—like irrationally annoy me, like beyond reason annoy me. On one level, I completely understand why car ad writers use certain catchphrases. On another level, though, I irrationally hate them. Here are the phrases along with my inner dialogue.

Ad Phrase: "The AC is cold as ice!"
Me: Have you ever touched ice?
Ad Phrase: "The transmission shifts like a dream!"
Me: Your dreams make me sad.
Ad phrase: "has potential"
Me: Great! That's exactly what I'm looking for in a vehicle—something that I can possibly, maybe, sorta, kinda, perhaps, someday drive—*potentially.*
Ad phrase: "mostly highway miles"
Me: Sure they are. Liar! I'm sure you use your car to drive exclusively between cities whilst hopping onto your scooter every time you need to drive within the city limits. You're such a hipster.

When I decided to list our van for sale, I was determined to avoid all these phrases. Of course, avoiding half those phrases wasn't going to be a problem, mainly because our transmission seemingly controlled our AC. And due to this issue, our AC—rather than being cold as ice—was cold enough to melt ice.

Highway Miles

My wife and I love each other dearly. We have a lot of fun and a lot of grand adventures. We don't argue very much—even when our grand adventures lead us into rather precarious situations. However, if you put us in the car together—me as the driver and her as the navigator—and if you tell us to drive to a location that isn't terribly easy to find, things don't end well. I'm neither confirming nor denying anything, but it's possible that I only listen to half of the directions she gives me. You see, I'm easily distracted by conversation—usually my own internal dialogue with myself, where I ponder the deeper things in life (for example, why is it that I can remember almost all the lyrics to Coolio's "Gangsta's Paradise" from 1995 but can't remember where I put my phone 30 seconds ago?). Additionally, it is possible that Careese only gives me about half of the necessary directions because she spends a significant amount of time turned backward, taking care of whatever snack or entertainment emergencies are going on in the kid cargo hold or talking to Mary about who knows what. Anyhow, we often miss turns or exits, and all five of our love languages rapidly descend into sarcasm. Perhaps you and your spouse can relate.

Me: "Which exit do we take?"

My lovely wife: "Let me check [checks GPS]. Oh, we were supposed to take the exit back there—the one we just passed."

Me: "You had one job, navigatrix."

My lovely wife: "I told you five miles ago to watch for that exit, and you said, 'Got it.'"

Me: "I don't think that conversation happened."

My lovely wife: "It did."

Me: "Pretty sure it didn't."

Me: [vaguely recalls the conversation but refuses to admit it]

Awkward silence.

My lovely wife: "Fine. I'm done. You figure it out."

Me: "I would love to, but I'm driving and shouldn't be on my phone while I'm driving."

My lovely wife: "Pull the van over and figure it out, then. I'll be reading my book."

What's that? You and your spouse don't get into arguments on road trips? Only us? Well, this is awkward. Pray for us.

Anyhow, the preceding conversation was pretty much the setting as we were running late to my cousin Candice's wedding in rural Oklahoma. My wife had delegated her navigatrix role to Siri. Even though Siri's directions sounded ridiculous, I followed them anyway. At some point, Siri decided to deceive me (or—and this is highly unlikely—I got confused and made a wrong turn). Fortunately, Careese took pity on me, jumped back into her navigatrix role, and spotted a sign for the road where we were supposed to turn. I turned Siri off and headed for the road. The paved road turned into a dirt road. A car passed us going in the other direction, so I figured we were getting close to our destination. A couple miles later, we crossed a bumpy metal cattle guard. Before we knew it, we found ourselves in the middle of a cow pasture in the middle of nowhere in the middle of rural Oklahoma. There were cows. There was no wedding. Oops. I surmised that the car we had passed on the dirt road was another husband-wife driving duo who had made the same mistake, which made me feel a little better about my driving choices.

The wedding was due to start in a matter of minutes. We frantically searched Google until we found the address for the wedding venue and humbly asked Siri back into our life. Ten or 15 minutes of frantic, semi-traffic-law-obedient driving later, we arrived. The wedding was at a beautiful outdoor venue. We were already on edge due to our tardiness when we realized we had another problem. Not only had the wedding begun, but the seating for the event was just a hundred or so yards from the grass field that was serving as the parking lot. Any sound coming from the parking lot—including a giant van and its inhabitants—would be heard by all the punctual wedding attendees. We implored our children to remain silent when they exited the van so we wouldn't disturb the wedding, but we knew the challenge awaiting us. Kids can be fast, or kids can be quiet. They cannot be both. We sped into a parking spot, frantically unbuckled all the car seats, and started fast-walking to the wedding. We opted for a moderately fast, moderately quiet pace—with a steady cadence of shushing along the way. We tried to sneak into one of the back rows so no one would notice we were late. We're a family of 11. Everyone heard us coming. Everyone noticed we were late. Sorry, cousin.

Fortunately, the story had a happy ending. The second half of the wedding was beautiful. Of course, I'm sure that the beginning of the wedding was equally lovely, but we were busy navigating our way out of a cow pasture. The reception afterward was incredible. If there's one thing my kids love more than just about anything else in the world, it's a reception where there's cake and dancing. Play the Cupid Shuffle, and the Wood kids will love you for life. They were not disappointed. There was cake. There was dancing. There was the Cupid Shuffle. We all danced until the music stopped playing—and a bit after.

Before I move on, I need to make sure you have an accurate picture in your mind. You might be envisioning my wife, me, and our nine kids performing a perfectly choreographed, Jackson-5-ish dance to every song while an adoring audience looks on in amazement. Inaccurate. I'm a financial planning nerd who loves numbers and spreadsheets. I dance exactly like that. My wife has some rhythm, and our kids are a solid blend of the two of us. Some of our kids have my wife's rhythm. Some of our kids have mine. One of our kids has my dance skills and my wife's boldness. It's truly something to behold. It's like his hips don't lie, but they should. Fortunately, no one judged us for our dancing atrocities. Better yet, no one judged us for being late to the wedding in the first place. God bless you, Wood family. You're the best.

Farm Van

After the ad for the van went viral and I began fielding questions from interested buyers from all over the country, one thing surprised me. Not one person asked about the van's time at the farm. To be fair, it was a seemingly innocuous line in the ad: "We've been using this van as our farm van for the past year or so." But if there was one line in the ad that begged for more disclosure, it was this one. Allow me to explain.

After a long and brutal life of road trips, we retired the Struggle Bus to our farm—the same Christmas light farm you read about in Chapter 3. Our van eased into retirement with small workloads, hauling small-ish loads of lights, extension cords, and props around the 10 acres. The bench seats remained empty in case we needed to haul people as well as junk. It was a simple and happy way for the van to live out its twilight years.

Then something happened. Perhaps you've seen the TV show *Hoarders*. In the off chance that you haven't, here's a brief synopsis. It's a reality show that highlights people who have turned their homes into abominable hoards of junk. Often, a tragic and traumatic event served as a catalyst for the person's slow accumulation of various items and a subsequent inability to part with said items. Over a period of years or even decades, this hoarding gradually turned his or her home into a massive hoard of trash, souvenirs, trinkets, clothing, and junk. In severe cases, the hoarding problem extends into the world of food and pets. In those cases, the hoarding problem has become a health hazard, and the people with the hoarding problem have become a danger to themselves and others.

In the show, it took most people many years to reach the extreme levels of depravity that led to being featured on *Hoarders*. Our Struggle Bus reached a similar level of depravity in about two weeks. I don't even know how it happened. One day, I was loading the back of the van with a dozen boxes of multicolor Christmas lights and loading the kids in the van for a quick drive out to the farm. The next day, I was saying things like, "Sorry, kids. I know it looks like there's room for one more person here, but there's not. I have to put the chickens in that seat."

The van was packed full of tools, lights, snacks, empty egg cartons, water bottles, rope, stakes, adhesive tapes of many kinds (duct, electrical, vinyl, etc.), two-by-fours, nails, screws, and anything else you can imagine. One thing that always fascinated me about the show *Hoarders* was that many of the hoarders always seemed to know exactly where to find random items in their hoard. They may have been divorced from reality in a lot of ways, but their spatial reasoning was on point.

Relative of hoarder: "How can you find anything in here? Suppose I asked to borrow a stapler. Would you know where to find one?"

Hoarder: "Sure! It's in the guest bedroom beside cat bed #4. It's on top of the 1997 editions of the *New York Times* but underneath the cheese grater."

How could someone with a possible mental disorder have such a fantastic memory? It never made sense to me. Now, though, I totally understood. If anyone other than I were to have opened the door to our van, he or she would have seen an indescribable and completely unorganized mess of chaos. (Well, they would see this assuming the hoard did not pour out of the van and crush him or her under the weight of its violent disgustingness.) I saw the hoard differently, though. The whole thing was mapped out in my brain.

Need a snack? No problem! There's a granola bar between the seats. Just move the egg cartons and bag of tools out of the way.

Need a box of 100 warm-white LED lights? No problem! They are located in the first bench seat underneath the red lights, shovel, level, rope, and inflatable snowman.

Chicken pooped on your shirt? No problem! I've got a spare shirt in a Walmart bag. Look under the pile of extension cords under the second bench seat. Oh, but be careful not to spill the box of nails, screws, and bolts. Would you grab me a bottle of water while you're back there?

I empathized with the hoarders. There was no room for anyone to ride in the van with me anymore, but that was okay. I was becoming friends with my hoard. We understood each other. We got along great. We bonded (sometimes literally, thanks to copious amounts of caulk, Gorilla Glue, and duct tape I had hoarded).

After we sold the farm, the time came to de-hoard the van. Much like the individuals on *Hoarders*, I couldn't do it initially. Facing your own depravity is depressing. Also, dehoarding takes a lot more work than creating the hoard. But when we decided to sell the van, I had no choice. I had to face reality.

But I didn't face reality. Over the course of a week, my sweet wife cleaned out the entire van by herself while I was at work. I think she knew how dehoarding was going to go down had I been there to help. It would have gone down exactly like hoarder confrontations go down on the TV show.

Careese: "Shovel. Keep it or throw it away?"
Me: "Keep it, of course."

Careese: "I shouldn't have to ask, but the used plastic spoon from the McFlurry you ate last year, keep it or throw it away?"

Me: "Keep it. You can't find spoons like that anymore."

Careese: "Broken strand of 50 lights. Keep it or throw it away?"

Me: "Keep it. I can fix those."

Careese: "Eight thousand more broken strands of lights. Keep them or throw them away?"

Me: "Keep them. I'll fix them all someday. Keep everything! We may need this stuff someday."

My wife is great like that. If it weren't for her, the van would probably still be sitting in my driveway, functioning as a mobile storage unit, waiting for TLC network to show up on my doorstep with TV cameras, a licensed psychologist, and some hazmat suits.

"Then the LORD God said, 'It is not good that the man should be alone; I will make him a helper fit for him" (Gen. 2:18).

I agree with God. If you've made it this far into the book, I bet that—at least my case—you agree as well. It would not be good for me to be alone. God knew I needed a helper, and not in the passive, acquiescent, flattering, or subservient sense of the word. No, I needed a helper in the original Hebrew biblical sense of the word. Throughout the Old Testament, the Hebrew word for helper (*ezer*) used in Genesis 2:18 refers to God as a helper to humanity.[1] Additionally, the Hebrew word for help is used in the context of military alliance and reinforcement. What does this context tell me? It tells me that God didn't create Eve because Adam needed a trusty sidekick to help him name the animals or build a tree fort or declutter his man cave or do his laundry or make him sandwiches. He didn't need a navigatrix for cross-garden of Eden road trips or a does-this-fig-leaf-spark-joy? questioning sidekick to prevent him from becoming the world's first hoarder. No, what Adam needed—what humans needed—was a military-grade ally to bring military-grade reinforcement in a divinely inspired way. Because parenting is messy. Because life is messy.

There have been seasons in life when I've foolishly treated my wife as though my life plans mattered more than her life plans. During these seasons,

---

1. James Strong, *Strong's Concordance*, Blue Letter Bible, 1986, 11.

I acted as though she was created to be my helper in a passive, trusty-sidekick kind of way—like a Robin to my Batman. Like a passenger seat navigatrix to my driver's seat trip commander. Almost 17 years of marriage and 15 years of parenting in the trenches have taught me this: wives were not meant to be resigned to the passenger seats of life. I don't believe that was God's design or the biblical meaning of the word *helper*. I think that's why so much tension is created when husbands assume a role of an authoritative delegator, placing themselves in the driver's seat of life as the czar of the family while relegating their wives to the role of the ever-subservient passenger seat navigatrix.

Worse, sometimes husbands—myself included—don't allow their wives a seat in the car (or van, as it were) at all. Instead, we keep secrets. We create literal (as in the case of our farm van) and figurative hoards of depravity. Then, in an attempt to shelter our wives or ourselves from pain, we try to keep those hoards secret. We don't allow them to help. That was not God's design either. It is not good for man to be alone. . .or to deal with hoards of depravity alone.

Life is better with military-grade reinforcement, not side-kick subservience. To navigate the back roads of life. To lovingly confront our messes. To go to battle with us and for us in the literal and figurative trenches of the hoards of depravity in our lives. It is not good for man to be alone.

CHAPTER 13
FRT

Q: *"Is the registration current?"*

*A: Yes! It should be noted, however, that the first three letters
of the current license plate are FRT. We have five boys under the age
of 12 in our house. This is a very unfortunate combination.*

In the state of Texas, there is a requirement that your car be inspected (and pass said inspection) before the state allows you to renew your car's registration. When it came time to renew the van's registration, I procrastinated. If you've managed to read this far into this book, you know why.

Definition of inspection: noun. a checking or testing of an individual against established standards.

I was 72 percent sure the van would meet the "established standards" for operational functionality, but I was 100 percent positive it would not meet the established societal standards for cleanliness, smell, or human dignity. Getting the van inspected would involve turning over the keys to a service center employee. I was certain this employee would never look at me the same way again. I didn't know exactly what words he or she would use to judge me, but I guessed they would be similar to what follows.

"Well, sir. Your van has failed the state inspection. While it seems to meet the requirements mechanically, you've reached a level of van hoarding that qualifies you for a reality show. You disgust me. May God have mercy on your soul. That'll be $15."

So, I procrastinated. I waited a couple months past the registration due date before I boldly drove to my favorite local car inspection joint: Toot'n

Totum. Yes, you read that correctly. Toot'n Totum. I pulled up to the Toot'n Totum car care center. There was one other car being tended to. I don't remember what kind of car it was, but it was nice and shiny and new. In other words, it was basically the opposite of my van. Out came the employee. My first thought: "You, sir, have just lost the car inspection lottery. I pity you." To his credit, he didn't judge me—at least not to my face. I explained the reason for my visit, apologized for any communicable diseases he might be subjected to, and handed him the keys. A while later, he returned with my keys and delivered the good news: the Struggle Bus had passed inspection. He spoke few words as he delivered the news, and I detected a look of righteous judgment in his eyes along with another more communicative look. It was a look that two men sometimes give each other, a look that, without words, communicates a mutual pact—a look that says, "Let's never speak of this again." I accepted my silent judgment. The van had passed inspection; I had not, either as a driver or as a man. But the deed was done.

With the state inspection behind me, I was finally legally eligible to renew my state registration. I drove to the county tax office, paid my fee, apologized for my tardiness, and was presented with an envelope containing two new license plates. When I arrived at home, I opened the envelope. I immediately noticed the first three letters: FRT. I almost hopped back into the van, returned to the Randall County tax office, and asked for replacement plates. Then I remembered the kind lady who had handed me my license plates. Did I really want to explain to her my reason for returning the plates? What if she was naïve, innocent, or kid-less? What if my large family had skewed my reality and I was making something out of nothing? What if she didn't understand and I had to spell it out for her in front of an audience of Randall County tax office patrons? It would make for an extremely awkward conversation.

Me: "Excuse me, ma'am. I know I was just issued these plates, but I would like to return them and request new ones."

"Why?" she would ask.

"Well, as you can see, the first three letters are FRT," I would reply.

Innocent lady: "Yes, that is correct. What's the problem?"

Me: "You know, um, FRT. It sounds like the word for flatulence."

Innocent lady: "Ew, gross! What is wrong with you?"

Ultimately, I decided the odds were in my favor. After all, FRT humor is inborn. Surely the Randall County tax office would sympathize with my predicament. I opted to return the plates, engage in awkward conversation, and ask for replacements. Unfortunately, by the time I had made my decision, the tax office was closed for the day. So I decided to drive back to the tax office on a day when I had an hour to spare. Never happened. In hindsight, I think fate was rooting for an FRT license plate to grace the back side of the Struggle Bus. Fate won.

In the months after I received my plates, I discovered that Randall County, Texas, must have lost the Texas state license plate distribution lottery. There are FRT license plates all over our city. Actually, I think I know what happened. I'm betting that a devious state employee hatched a plot to put all the FRT license plates in the part of the state where vehicle owners would predominately be filling up their vehicles with gas at convenience stores named Toot'n Totum. Well, Mr. State Employee, your devious plot was a resounding success. FRT cars, FRT vans, and FRT trucks all over Amarillo are pulling into Toot'n Totums to fill up with gas. The plates are an annoyance to us parents but a hero to our city's children. My boys are grateful.

Of course, when you have as many kids as we do, a license plate that begins with the letters FRT is really the least of your objectionable humor-related worries. Grossness abounds in the houses of large families.

Nature versus nurture. That is a huge debate in the world of parenting. Is the behavior of children determined by their environment, or is it more of an inborn quality? As a parent, you quickly learn that there is merit to both sides of the argument. Some behaviors are learned. Some behaviors are inborn. I've discovered a universal truth regarding this debate. Nature is strong. Nature is powerful. And here's the deal. Nature thinks toots are funny. There's simply no way to train a child otherwise. We have a lot of kids, which means we have a lot of tooters, which means we have a lot of toot-related laughter, which means we have a lot of times when I say things like, "Stop it! That's gross! We don't do that at the dinner table," while simultaneously trying to be a respectable adult and stifle my own laughter.

Have you ever had to tell your toddler, "Ew, gross! No! Never, never lick a toilet"? We have. Twice. Now, though, we have a family full of non-toilet-lickers. Nurture matters.

You know how some kids as toddlers insist on shoving anything and everything into their mouths? We had one such kid. It was a constant battle. Before he was able to walk, he crawled on the floor with his tongue dangling out of his mouth and dragging against the floor as his breath and saliva steam mopped our house. He would gobble up anything in his path. We were constantly watching and quick to act, but he was sometimes quicker. Sand. Glitter. A marble. We found all three in the business end of his diaper on different occasions. Nature compels kids to taste things. Nurture compels them to stop licking the dang floor.

Kids are gross. It's their nature.

One day, my wife walked into the bathroom to witness our four-year-old son standing on top of the tank of the toilet whilst attempting to pee into the bowl down below. It would have been more funny than awful if he hadn't had his hands on his hips whilst swiveling them in a circular motion. As best we could tell, he was trying to maximize the splash effect. His accuracy was less than 20 percent. It was like a war zone in there. Fortunately, God made bleach.

Kids are gross. It's their nature.

Me to our four-year-old (knowing we didn't have any peanuts in our pantry): "Where did you get that peanut from?"

Four-year-old: "From under the couch."

Me: "It's really gross to eat things from under the couch!"

Four-year-old: "But I got all the hair off of it."

Kids are gross. It's their nature.

I put our almost-three-year-old son in our shower. There was a variety of toys for him to play with in the shower. One of the toys was a tiny toilet from our girls' Barbie dollhouse. As I pulled him out of the shower, I noticed a little pile of poop adjacent to the Barbie toilet. He had attempted to use the tiny toilet. He missed. Nurture teaches a child about appropriate repositories for poop, but it is important to be very specific.

I once walked into the bathroom to find a soaking wet roll of toilet paper on top of the toilet. I walked into the living room to find the toilet's most recent toddler user sucking her thumb.

Kids are gross. It's their nature.

Our daughter had just turned three, and we had just watched the classic Walt Disney movie *Bambi*. Daughter: "Sometimes my bottom sounds like Thumper."

Kids are. . .observant.

Our five-year-old was taking longer than he should have in the bathroom. I knocked on the door and asked, "Are you almost done in there? Are you okay?"

He replied with an overly grunty voice, "I got two poops out, but I have three more in there."

Me: "How do you even know. . .never mind. . .just hurry it up in there."

On another occasion, we walked into the bathroom to check on our almost-three-year-old. He said, "Mommy, I'm not done yet." He holds up five fingers and, starting with his pinky, begins to count them. "I got one, two, three, four poops out." Then he points to his thumb. "But this one's not out yet."

Sometimes kids are more in tune with nature than I am.

Of course, as a parent, the grossness that happens in the confines of your home isn't really the issue, is it? No, it's trying to pretend to the outside world that nothing gross happens in your home. We want the world to think we've got this whole nurture thing figured out. When my four-year-old eats a hairy peanut from under the couch, I'm disturbed, but I'm not embarrassed. No one was there to judge me. No, as a parent, it's the public grossness that gets you. It's those moments when, in public, the world catches a glimpse of your family's depravity and acts like no one in their home has ever peed on a wall or eaten dog food. It's when the world judges your nurturing ability and finds you lacking. Nurture-shaming. Those are the low moments.

When our kids were young, I played on a church softball league. Our kids had come out to watch me play and were crawling around on the bleachers, as kids do. We looked over and noticed that our four-year-old was chewing gum. "Where did you get gum?" his mom asked. Happily, my son pointed under the bleachers. "From under there. There's a lot of it there!" Nurture-shamed.

We were sitting in a church service with our three-year-old daughter. The time came for communion. The whole room had gone silent as the congregation paused to reflect on the deeper meaning of the sacrament. Every head was bowed, and every eye was closed. My daughter chose this moment—the quietest moment of the entire service—to blurt out, "DADDY! I HAVE A WEDGIE!" Every head was no longer bowed, and every eye was no longer closed. Sorry, Jesus. My daughter was both in church and wearing underwear. I thought I was doing pretty well with this whole nurture thing. Didn't matter. Nurture-shamed.

In 2014, we took our kids on the lowest budget cruise we could find. It departed from Galveston, Texas. From the animal-shaped towels left on freshly made beds to the unlimited supply of food to the 24/7 room service, the cruise was awesome. One of the highlights of our cruisin' time was the staff. They were delightful. In case you've never been on a cruise, here's how it works. You are served by an army of people over the course of your time on the boat, but you are paired with one dinner server for the duration of your stay. He or she serves your dinner to you each night of the cruise. On this particular cruise, our server's name was Bam Bang (pronounced Bahm Bahng). Bam Bang ruled, and not just because he had the greatest name ever.

One night during dinner, all the servers put on a mid-meal show of coordinated singing and dancing. They danced around, hopped up on tables, twirled their towels, and sang to the music. It was a ton of fun. Bam Bang, despite being slightly rhythmically challenged, was right there in the midst of the revelry, dancing it up like no one was watching. We applauded him mightily. About midway through the song and dance number, I noticed that the attention of a few of my kids was drifting from the singing and dancing fun to the table next to us. Since the beginning of the meal, I had been trying to distract them from this very table. You see, the table next to us was packed with middle-aged women who had spent the prior hour increasing their blood alcohol levels as quickly and merrily as possible. Their language had been gradually growing more colorful, and their volume was reaching a crescendo. Have you heard the term "WOO girls"? This was an entire table full of inebriated WOO girls. Their server reached the point in the choreography where he hopped up on the table to dance. I didn't exactly know what was coming, but I knew that WOO girls + alcohol + table dancing was not the math I wanted my family full of young kids to witness.

True to form, several of the women started shouting "WOO!" Then, as if they had been saving them for this very occasion, they each pulled wads of dollar bills out of their purses and pockets. Into their server's pants went their hands and dollar bills. Their server, who was clearly not expecting such treatment, thanked them awkwardly, stepped down from the table, and continued dancing. I tried to distract my children to no avail. The raucous song of the drunken WOO girls was unignorable. I looked over at my seven-year-old son. As he twirled his towel over his head, he shouted, with all the wonderful innocence of a seven-year-old, "HEY, MOMMY! CAN WE HAVE SOME DOLLAR BILLS? DID YOU BRING ANY FOR US TO GIVE TO BAM BANG?" And Bam Bang quickly danced himself away from our table. Praise God none of our children happened to be carrying any cash. Otherwise, we would've never been able to make eye contact with Bam Bang again. Also, I think the WOO girls mostly succeeded in distracting the other tables around us from the fact that our seven-year-old was asking for dollar bills to tip the table dancers. We imparted a valuable life lesson to our kids that day. Whether on cruise ships or in life, there will never be an appropriate time to shove dollar bills into someone's pants. Nature tells you it's okay to act as the adults around you are acting. Nurture's job: remind nature that adults are often idiots.

Nurture-shamed by Bam Bang.

One time, we were standing in line at McDonald's, waiting patiently for our turn to place our order. Out of nowhere, our four-year-old pointed at the lady directly in front of us in line and asked, "Daddy, did Jesus make that lady fat?"

Nurture-shamed.

One lovely day in early fall I was sitting in my living room and heard the siren song of the ice cream truck. I laughed to myself about a recent conversation between my wife and me about one particularly creepy ice cream man we'd encountered who—well—I'll put it this way. He reeked of illegality (at least in 40 states) and needed to reexamine his life and career choices. My six-year-old was playing in the front yard, and I was watching through the front window. The ice cream truck came to a stop in front of our house. My daughter, keeping a cautious distance between herself and the truck, said something to him. He immediately drove away. She then came inside, noticing that I had been watching out the front window.

"Daddy, I told him that Mommy wouldn't let us buy any ice cream because he creeps her out."

Oops. Apparently, our conversation wasn't as private as we thought.

Nurture-shamed by the ice cream truck driver.

The more I've talked with parents over the years, the more I've realized that we're all in this together. As much as we all pretend we have it together, we don't. We post our nurturing highlight reels to social media, but we're messily battling nature. Our sons have terrible toilet accuracy. Our daughters laugh at toots. We're all out here trying our best to raise proper humans in the midst of the grossness. So don't judge other people's parenting by the gross or moderately inappropriate things their kids say or do in public. Nurturing is hard. We're trying our best.

I feel as though I should end this chapter with an important nature-nurture-related public service announcement—a bit of unsolicited advice about unsolicited advice. The desire to pass along our nurturing advice is ingrained in our nature. We want to help. We want to teach. But sometimes we need to defy our nature. There's a time and a place for helping, teaching, admonishing, and co-nurturing. Do you know when and where that time and place is not? The grocery store checkout line. There seems to be some mystical force that hovers over said grocery store checkout line. It calls to all who enter it unaccompanied by children. I have no proof of this, but I think the voice calls in the voice of Gollum from *The Lord of the Rings*. "They needs it. They wants it. Nurture-shame them, my precious. Give thems the advice. Give thems the shame."

The grocery store line is a terrible place to evangelize your message of proper parenting. Sometimes little kids are going to do gross or moderately inappropriate things in the checkout line. Our kids are wonderfully well-behaved (yes, I'm biased, but I'm not lying), but we've had many such incidents. We parents are trying to unload our carts and go through the checkout process as fast as possible whilst simultaneously keeping our kids from licking the floor, grabbing all the eye-level toys and candy, and morphing into cart-confined, nap-deprived rage monsters. Do you know what thought has never once crossed my mind? This one: "I can't seem to get my kid to stop crying or grabbing Twix bars. I bet the stranger behind me has some sage parenting wisdom. I hope they start blurting it out, because I'm too shy to ask. That'd be fantastic!" No, this is not the time for your 20-minute treatise on proper discipline and care of a child. If you want to help, use less phrases that begin with "back in my day" and more phrases that begin with "let me pay for all your stuff!"

Sincerely,
Parents everywhere

CHAPTER 14
THE RECOMMENDATION OF PROFESSIONAL HELP

I recommend getting this thing checked over by a mechanic before buying.
Everything under the hood looks and sounds fine to me, but then again,
I would have no idea if it didn't look or sound right.

. . .

I don't want to paint with a broad brush here, but every single
contractor in the world is a miserable, incompetent thief.

—Ron Swanson

Young Josh was the type of person who was opposed to professional help. Contractors. Accountants. Doctors. Plumbers. Lawyers. Realtors. I'm embarrassed to admit that young Josh avoided them all. My thought was, why should I pay the exorbitant fees of a professional when I live in a world where I have access to Google? Time and time again, I discovered that spending 20 minutes on Google or YouTube did not make me as knowledgeable as someone who had spent a decade or two in the profession. Shocking.

Older Josh has seen the light. Sure, some professionals are incompetent thieves, but professionals have overwhelmingly been a God-send to our family. The remainder of this chapter will be devoted to honoring the dear professionals who've waded into our Struggle Bus life and provided help when we needed it most.

Plumbers

Salespeople often speak of going after a "whale"—a customer so huge that he or she can make or break a salesperson's entire year or even career. Plumbers, the Wood family is your whale. Plumbers have saved us on countless occasions. In addition to normal, run-of-the-mill plumbing issues such as water heater problems and leaky pipes, large families like ours are the geese that never stop laying the golden eggs of plumbing catastrophes.

One time, plumbers came to the rescue when the toilet was overflowing and no amount of plunging was doing the trick. It is worth noting that my wife and I are expert plungers. We earned all-state honors in 2007. This time, though, no luck. Unplungeable. What did the plumbers find? A pipe crammed full of non-flushable baby wipes. When we questioned the kids, we discovered that one of them (who shall remain nameless) was using them exclusively for number-two-related business because, and I quote, "They felt nice."

Another time, the same toilet became unplungeable again. Additionally, the sink next to the toilet was clogged. This time, between the two, the plumbers found a marble, a small action figure, part of a granola bar wrapper, remnants of a cardboard roll of toilet paper, a Q-tip, a Lego brick, and the entire payload of one of those wax-melting scentsy things. It was such a ridiculous conglomeration of cloggers that one of the plumbers stopped to take a picture of the messy little pile. It was subsequently tacked to a plumbers' wall of fame that was created in our honor. Probably.

In our previous home, our sewer line kept backing up to the point that sewage began to fill our bathtub. I cannot overstate how gross we all found that to be. Also, remember the "law of parent fail amplification" from Chapter 3? A similar thing happened here. Do you want to guess how many of our friends, family, and total strangers in the checkout line at Walmart were told by our young children, "Hey! Our bathtub at home has poop in it"? The answer: all of them. Anyhow, after twice running a declogging contraption through the drain as well as depleting the dollar store's entire supply of discount drain cleaner, we called our plumber to run a camera through the line to see what the issue was. In addition to having a small root growing into our line, our toddler had crammed an uncapped clean-out valve with a variety of toys, sticks, rocks, and anything else he could fit in there. Additionally, the plumbers discovered that some dastardly squirrels had been dropping acorns down an uncovered vent pipe on our roof. We had a vent pipe full of acorns and a sewer line full of small toys. Like I said, plumbers, the Wood family is your whale.

During the winter of 2012, I left town for a few days for a work conference. Around 7:30 p.m. one evening, I called to check in on the kids and tell everyone good night. My wife answered the phone. I immediately began telling her about my day, how wonderful it had been, how much I'd learned, and how good the food was. My wife sat silently and listened until I asked, "So, how's your day going?"

"Well, the kids all have the flu. Not one of the kids. Not some of the kids. All of the kids have the flu. Four out of six of them have been vomiting all day. That's bad enough, but I tried to wash a load of vomit sheets and clothes and was unsuccessful because it's 12 degrees outside, and our pipes are frozen. Also, I'm pretty sure one of the pipes burst, but I won't know until it thaws. That should be fun. I can't wash our clothes or anything else. Also, I can't flush one of our toilets. So our house smells like death and looks like a war zone. You could say that my day is not going well. Tell me more about your luxury vacation."

I replied, "Stinks to be you!" and sent her a selfie of me in a hot tub eating lobster.

I'm kidding, of course. I value my life.

I felt terrible. There was nothing I could do to help. Thankfully, my dad and father-in-law leaped into action and started thawing the pipes. A team of plumbers arrived shortly thereafter and fixed one of the pipes in the wall that had, in fact, burst. Thanks, parents and plumbers.

Fast-forward one year. We decided to sell our home. During the home sale process, we discovered a leak. At this point in our lives, this was news that surprised exactly none of us. Water was leaking from a broken pipe located inside the slab foundation of our home. Would you like to know what it sounds like to have a leak in your foundation? Imagine the sound of a gaggle of plumbers salivating. It sounds exactly like that. Our plumber's golden goose had laid yet another golden egg. His plan to fix the leak was fascinating. It involved tunneling under the house, cutting through the slab from underneath the house, replacing the entire line, and backfilling the tunnel. This was the moment that I realized I should have chosen a career in plumbing. A very special shout-out to our insurance agent who had included a "slab leakage rider" in our policy. We owe you our gratitude and approximately $30,000.

Agents, Adjusters, and Arborists

We've owned three houses in Amarillo. Trees have fallen on all three of them. I don't know what the odds are of that happening, but they can't be good. We've been blessed by professional help every time.

House #1, tree #1: It was snowy outside. A teenage driver lost control of her car, sending her skidding into our yard and careening into one of the trees beside our house. She hit said tree just hard enough to knock it over and onto our house. Kids, please don't text and drive. It wasn't a huge tree (maybe 10 to 15 feet tall), but it still did a bit of damage to our siding. Insurance paid to fix everything. Thanks, insurance agents.

House #2, tree #2: I was at work when I received a phone call from my wife. "Our tree just fell on our Sequoia, and I can't get it out of the driveway."

"Okay, I'll run home and try to get it moved out of the way for you," I replied.

I didn't understand the gravity of the situation. My jaw dropped as I pulled up to our house. The largest tree in our front yard, which was at least 30 feet tall, had completely fallen over. Its trunk was at least two feet in diameter. Its branches and leaves completely covered our Sequoia, most of our yard, and some of our house. My I'll-be-the-hero-husband-and-move-it-out-of-the-way plan was not going to happen. I called a professional tree-trimming company. A small army of lumberjack-looking fellows armed with chainsaws and a massive wood chipper came to save the day. They let me toss a bunch of tree remnants into the wood chipper. I could've done that all day. I loved that thing. I was, unfortunately, strictly forbidden from throwing any other items into the wood chipper. "The husband always asks to throw random stuff in there. We aren't allowed to do it." Bummer. Oh well. Thanks, lumberjacks.

House #3, tree #3: It was a rather stormy night in Amarillo, and we had all just sprinted into the house from the van (the van doesn't fit in our garage). We had just walked into the kitchen when we heard a giant boom. The whole house shook. I walked outside and immediately smelled the distinct aroma of burning wood. It didn't take long to find the source of the boom and smell. Our yard, the street, and our neighbors' yards were littered with the shattered remains of a 30-foot cottonwood tree. This tree had, until a few minutes ago, stood in our front yard. Now, massive chunks of cottonwood lay on our roof and in our front yard. Did you know that lightning could shatter a tree? I did not. Several shards of the tree were sticking through our roof like little javelins. Our neighbors across the street removed a four-foot chunk of wood from their roof. All our neighbors had remnants of various sizes of our tree in their yards—both their front yards and backyards. It was one powerful explosion. Our house quickly became a temporary tourist attraction for the neighborhood as everyone searched for ground zero of the massive boom. We seized the opportunity to teach the kids a science, safety, and insurance lesson. By science, safety, and insurance lesson, I mean I walked around with the kids and said, "You see, kids, when electrons in the. . .OOOO! Would you look at that?. . .Whoa! That lightning blew the mess out of that branch!. . .Hey, look over there! PART OF OUR TREE IS STICKING OUT OF OUR ROOF! We could've died! Lightning is awesome! This is why we don't play with golf clubs when it's stormy. Also, the reason Daddy is able to marvel at the destruction rather than cry is because we have this thing called insurance."

A few days later, my kids all watched the insurance adjuster meticulously examine the scene and provide a report of the issues caused by the great cottonwood explosion. It was a bit like a crime scene investigation. Insurance adjusters don't exactly have the best reputation, but ours was great. He gave our home a thorough evaluation, adequately admired the God who created lightning, explained the process to us, and answered a socially acceptable level of the litany of questions my kids asked him. Thanks, insurance adjuster.

Realtors

Let's talk for a moment about selling a house. If you're a parent who is or will be selling a house, consider this my official endorsement of the realtor profession. If you're in the market to sell or buy a home, hire a knowledgeable real estate agent. You are too emotionally attached to some aspects of your home and too emotionally detached from others to accurately value your home. I've done the whole "for sale by owner" thing. I failed. I don't know how many hours I spent researching comps, spreadsheeting tax appraisals, conducting open houses, and generally stressing out about everything, but I'll put it this way. If I were to add up all those hours and multiply them by the current minimum wage of $7.25 per hour, it would equal more than what we would've paid in commission to a real estate agent (that's not as much of an exaggeration as I wish it were), and that's just the time I spent. I have no doubt I missed out on at least a couple thousand extra dollars in value by placing myself in the position of the haggle-ee. In hindsight, I'm pretty sure that potential buyers did not enjoy hearing my detailed stories of the days we spent joyfully destroying the resale value of our home.

"Funny story. . .that's the spot where I fell through the ceiling and landed on my car. That was immediately after yelling from the attic down to my wife, 'I'll be fine! I've been up here hundreds of times. I just have to make sure I stay on the beams and not accidentally. . .AHHH!'"

"Funny story. . .the fence pickets were a bit old. That's the spot where our dog rammed his head through the fence trying to greet a passerby."

"Funny story. . .I fixed those bricks myself after watching a YouTube video. You can barely tell that it wasn't done by a professional!" (You could tell.)

"Funny story. . .I got the electrical wires crossed when rewiring things. Unfortunately, this light switch controls the TV rather than the ceiling fan. Now that I've said it out loud, I realize there is no aspect of the previous sentence that is appealing to you as a potential buyer."

"Funny story. . .we accidentally bought the wrong kind of weed killer for our yard. So the whole yard is basically a dead man walking. You're going to need to reseed it."

And perhaps my all-time favorite. . .

"Funny story. . .the paint looks good now, but let me tell you a story."

Painters

Over the course of five days, I accidentally used six coats of paint on many of the walls of the house.

How on earth do you accidentally paint a wall six times? Thanks for asking.

Day 1: After a bit of pre-painting prep work (which I hate, by the way), I painted all the walls with white primer (coat #1). As soon as the primer was dry, I put on a coat of khaki-colored paint (coat #2). The walls appeared to be adequately covered after soaking up almost all my paint. I spent a couple minutes congratulating myself and marveling at my paint volume estimation ability. Then I called it a day, leaving the paint to dry overnight.

Day 2: When I walked in the next day, it was apparent that the previous day's version of Josh had been impaired by paint fumes or blind optimism or both. Every wall had an embarrassingly large number of areas that needed another coat of paint. I drove myself over to the paint store, bought more paint, headed back to the house, and repainted the many underpainted portions of the wall (coat #3).

Day 3: Armed with a tiny paintbrush, I walked back into the house to complete a few minor touch-ups and finish the job. Alas, Day 3 would not be a day for using my tiny brush. Every spot I had repainted the previous day appeared to be a shade darker than the rest of the wall. Every wall looked as though I (or a three-year-old) had attempted to paint a camouflage pattern and failed miserably. Apparently, the paint store employees had given me the wrong shade of paint. How could you have done this to me, paint store employees? What had I ever done to you?

I hopped in my car, armed with a bucket of mistinted paint and a larger bucket of unrighteous indignation.

In my head, I was bold and confrontational. As I began my drive to the paint store, I envisioned myself arriving, throwing open the door, flipping over a few paint tables (like Jesus flipping over the money changer tables) and launching into an impassioned speech rivaling Bill Pullman in *Independence Day* or William Wallace in *Braveheart.* I would close with "YOU CAN'T HANDLE THE TRUTH!" and the paint store manager, moved to tears and repentance by my speech, would begin to apologize profusely and bestow upon me a coupon for free paint for life.

In reality, though, real-life Josh is not one to cause a scene. I'm generally nonconfrontational. Also, Jesus tells me I'm not supposed to berate employees for their relatively minor mistakes. So I knew how the real-world scene was going to play out. I was going to walk up to the paint counter and be like, "Um, hey, I think you guys accidentally gave me the wrong paint color. Can you please fix it? I should have checked it before I left. It's my fault really, so, I'll totally understand if you can't give me a refund." Knowing this about real-life Josh, my thought process shifted from crafting a speech that would inspire a rebellion to simply trying to talk myself into standing firm enough to get free paint out of the deal.

Side note: Am I the only crazy person who does this?

Just as I was about to arrive at the store, the worst thing happened. Have you ever had one of those moments when you're furious with someone whose stupid mistake cost you both money and hours of your life only to realize that, in fact, you were the stupid one who made the stupid mistake? Yep, I had one of those moments. I was the one who had given the paint store employees the wrong paint color. The whole thing had been my mistake, not theirs. The worst. My rage quickly turned inward. I walked in, explained my mistake to the paint store employees, bought more paint, double-checked the color, drove back to the house, and repainted all the darker-shaded areas of the walls with a coat of rage and the correct shade of khaki (coat #4).

Day 4: I strutted into the house to admire a job done but not well done. I flipped on the light switch and began to cry. You see, as the light bounced off the walls, it was immediately obvious that coat #4 had a much shinier sheen than the previous coats of paint. The stupid walls were covered in stupid splotchy stupid patches of stupid semi-gloss paint. The color was spot on, but the sheen was not. Apparently, in my rage the previous day, I had rage-purchased semi-gloss paint instead of eggshell paint (the sheen of the previous coats). Kids, let this be a lesson to you. Rage-purchasing never ends well.

I headed back to the paint store again where I was now on a first-name basis with the employees. If you are old enough to have watched the classic show *Cheers*, you will remember how Norm was greeted by everyone at the bar every time he walked in. "NORM!" everyone said. I hadn't quite achieved Norm status at the paint store, but I was getting close. In fact, I felt a bit like ol' Norm.

It's a dog-eat-dog world, and I'm wearing Milk Bone underwear.

—Norm

On the bright side, I liked my new friends, and they liked my repeat business. Also worth noting: paint store employees are pretty solid grief counselors. Anyhow, I purchased all new paint—enough to coat all the walls twice.

Day 5: I finally mustered the energy to repaint all the walls. I started over. I painted two more coats of paint on every wall and touched everything up in one day (coats #5 and #6).

People often complain about how pricy it can be to hire a painter. Well, I've done a rough comparison. If I were to quantify my time, money, and mental anguish, I estimate the cost of my painting fiasco to be just north of $1.2 million. Hire a painter. The good ones are worth their money.

Lawyers

How many lawyer jokes are there? There are only two. The rest are true stories.
—Unknown

Throughout our adoption process, Careese and I were nervous wrecks. We felt powerless. It's one thing to laud our great country's system of government that is based on the rule of law. It's entirely another to sit back, watch, and pray that it functions properly because the fate of your children depends on it. Gut-wrenching. Foster parents and adoptive parents, you have our respect, our empathy, and our prayers. We watched our kids' state-appointed attorney navigate a mountain of legalese to fight for their best interest. Fortunately for us, God and the state of Texas decided that becoming a part of our crazy family was ultimately in their best interest. Sometimes, we question whether we're raising them the way they deserve. Well, every day we question it. But to this day, we pause to admire the kids' attorney. He fought fights we could not. He arranged a timetable we could not. He navigated a system we could not. Attorneys can be a blessing. We're forever thankful for ours.

Nurses

On our street lived a young boy with a BB gun. We lost many birds and a couple of windows due to said boy. The neighborhood was littered with his used BBs, which our kids thought to be a wonderful stroke of good fortune for our family. They spent hours hunting and collecting BBs as if they were as valuable as nuggets of gold. I chose not to inform them otherwise. Every day was like a tiny, time-consuming, parent-break-giving treasure hunt. During one such treasure hunt, one of our toddler sons discovered an unfortunate truth. A BB is intriguingly and temptingly close to the size of an ear hole. How close in size was it? In my son's mind, there was only one way to find out—shove that shiny sucker all up in there and see how well it fit. Spoiler alert: it fit like a glove.

My wife is super resourceful. She spent over an hour attempting to extract the BB through a variety of creative means—from tweezers to duct tape to suction power to a plethora of other "tools." Finally, she gave up and called our pediatrician's office.

"Hi, it's Careese Wood. [pause] Oh, I know, it has been a few weeks since we called! [pause] We've missed you, too. [pause] Well, today we have a BB lodged in an ear canal. [pause] I know, right? [pause] I agree, it is fun that they keep shaking things up so we don't get too bored. [pause] Thanks! I'll await the call."

A few minutes later a nurse called back. Rather than telling us to make a costly trip to the doctor's office, she gave Careese the recipe for a magical potion that could be gently dripped into the ear canal. If administered properly, the liquid would bubble up and push the BB out. As promised, after a few attempts, my wife succeeded in sciencing the BB out of our son's ear. Thanks, nurse.

Dentists

One Sunday afternoon, our two-year-old face-planted onto the brick step on our front porch. Both of his top front teeth were jammed into his gums. His bottom front teeth were loose. His lips were busted and rapidly swelling. While I was busy running around, freaking out and generally accomplishing nothing productive other than holding our wailing son, my wife called the after-hours emergency number for our dentist. Our dentist showed up on our front porch within a few minutes (yes, on a Sunday afternoon). She handled the whole situation (including two super-panicky parents) with amazing grace. We will forever appreciate her awesomeness.

Doctors

Do you know there is such a thing as a pediatric epileptologist? Me neither. . .until we needed one.

A little after 11:00 p.m. on a Monday night, Careese woke up our nine-year-old to have him use the bathroom before we went to bed. He was a bit disoriented and started walking the wrong way. Careese called him back toward the bathroom, and he started walking back in the right direction. When he had almost made it to the bathroom, his arms locked along with the rest of his body as he contracted into the fetal position and started convulsing. Careese held him as he continued convulsing and began foaming at the mouth. I called 9-1-1 and yelled our address at the poor, sweet 9-1-1 operator lady. (Sorry, lady. You were great. I was not.). After a couple minutes or so of convulsing, our son had still not resumed breathing and went completely limp. Unresponsive. We turned his head to drain his mouth and nose, checked for a pulse, and yell-cry-prayed as his lips and face turned pale and blue. It felt like an eternity. Finally, he took a breath, and his eyes opened. He continued breathing lightly but stared off into space, unblinking and unresponsive to anything cognitively. We counted out his breaths to the 9-1-1 operator. About that time, the ambulance showed up. Amarillo EMS, I love you and your rapid response time. He remained seemingly comatose until we were about halfway to the hospital. He still couldn't make eye contact or acknowledge my voice (or anyone else's), but he began to cry. He was scared, which gave me much relief that his little brain was functioning again. Not too long after that, he slowly regained his faculties. First, he was able to very softly answer no when the EMT asked if he was in pain. After an hour or so in the emergency room, he was able to make eye contact again, recognizing us and his grandparents. He started speaking again not long after that.

The next 24 hours were a blurry barrage of tests—blood tests, EKG, MRI, EEG, CAT scan, and more. He didn't get to sleep until about 5:30 a.m. but was quite the little trooper throughout all the poking, prodding, sticking, and questioning.

Thankfully, all tests but the EEG came back normal. Since his EEG came back abnormal, we spent another day at the hospital before being released Wednesday morning. No diagnosis was made, but the terms "absence seizures," "petit grand mal seizures," and "grand mal seizures" were used. We were told that our next stop would be a neurologist's office where we would get more information about the EEG and search for a diagnosis. We left the hospital hopeful and prayerful that the neurologist would help us with a diagnosis and subsequent plan for treatment. In the meantime, we were prescribed seizure medication.

Careese called our pediatrician Thursday morning to see where we stood on the scheduling of the neurologist appointment. She was told that the first available appointment to see a neurologist in Amarillo, Lubbock, or Dallas-Fort Worth was in May, five months away. If you know the God we serve or the wife I love, you'll know how the following little miracle happened. Within a few hours, we had two neurologist appointments scheduled—one in Amarillo the same afternoon and one with a pediatric neurologist in Fort Worth the following afternoon.

In the subsequent months, we met with a battery of doctors and specialists, including a pediatric epileptologist. He gave us a well-researched treatment plan and took the time to answer our numerous questions. I've never had a greater appreciation for medical professionals in my life.

As far as doctors, attorneys, real estate agents, insurance agents, insurance adjusters, arborists, plumbers, and other professionals go, some are crooks. Some are terrible. Some spend more on supplies and overhead than they should. Some are jerks. Some are terrible at their jobs. Some forget important details. But I've come to the following conclusion: those people are in the minority. The majority of professionals are individuals working hard to make an honest living. My experience has been that there's a far better chance of successful task completion when I use a professional rather than attempting things myself. The last time I attempted a home renovation project, I visited Home Depot or Lowe's 147 times in two days.

Ultimately, that's the role of professionals, to reduce the struggle or potential for struggle in our lives. None of us have the time for additional struggles. My advice for you is the same advice I gave the new owner of our Struggle Bus. Reduce the potential for struggle in your life by hiring a professional. Hire a mechanic. Hire a real estate agent. See a doctor. Hire a plumber. Will you sometimes spend more money than you should? Sure. Mostly, though, professionals will make your car, your house, and your life far less struggle-y and add far more value than what they'll charge.

Oh, and take all the money and time I just saved you, rent a wood-chipper, and spend a weekend tossing junk into it. Thank me later.

Conclusion

Walk a mile in my shoes and you'd be crazy too.

—Tupac

Writing this book has been quite the adventure. I spent hours digging through old photos, sifting through old memories, and reminiscing about days gone by with Careese and the kids. We've re-laughed, re-stressed, and re-loved our hoards of memories over and over again. This process has given me a newfound appreciation for that old Struggle Bus we sold and a peace about the issues our current van is having (it's already well on its way to becoming Struggle Bus 2.0). And it has given me an excitement about all the adventures that are still to come in whatever Struggle Bus we may own in the future. The struggle was, is, and always will be real. We wouldn't have it any other way. That said, I've decided to close this book with a few thoughts on the past, the present, and the future.

The Past

Never throughout history has a man who lived a life of ease left a name worth remembering.[1]

—Theodore Roosevelt

Throughout this book-writing process, I've worked to unearth our van's history, stories, and depravities in an effort to (1) preserve them for future generations of the Wood family and (2) hopefully bring a bit of laughter to the world. In essence, I'm a historian, albeit a terrible one who is overly

---

1. "Theodore Roosevelt Quotes," *Goodreads*, https://www.goodreads.com/quotes/133593 -never-throughout-history-has-a-man-who-lived-a-life.

focused on a single, ridiculous, depraved, vehicular piece of 2005 Americana. On second thought, what if I'm not a terrible historian? What if, say, in the year 2050—a year when all vehicles will surely be fully automated, flying, self-cleaning, self-driving, and self-de-chicken-nuggeting—a team of archaeologists unearths the ol' Struggle Bus and comes to the following conclusion: Our 2005 Ford E350 Extended Passenger van's struggles served as a catalyst that prompted more societal vehicular improvements than Elon Musk.

I take it back. I'm a great historian. You're welcome, people of year 2050.

Truthfully, writing the last 14 chapters has given me a new respect for real historians and archaeologists. I managed to pull 47,341 words worth of stories out of one broken-down van. I can't imagine how hard it would be to sift through and document the untold masses of stories contained in actual pieces of history, like the Great Pyramids or something. Here's to you, historians and archaeologists.

On the other hand, I do sometimes wonder what things archaeologists got completely wrong about history simply because they happened to excavate the home of a historical anomaly. For example, what if the picture we have of ancient Egyptian civilization is wrong because, by an unfortunate stroke of bad luck, archaeologists happened upon and excavated the home of a weird, struggle-chariot-driving, homeschooling Egyptian family of 11 rather than the home of the culturally normal family who resided across the street? I imagine them unearthing an ancient struggle chariot and writing a report similar to the following:

> Based on our findings, ancient Egyptian society consisted of numerically large, unhygienic families. It appears that families of the time stored their chicken nuggets, trash, spare clothing, and toys in rusty holes in the backs of their chariots. Our best guess is that they did this for easy access. Clearly, Egyptian society had a very poor understanding of the importance of sanitation. Life expectancy of the time was surprisingly low, and we're beginning to understand why. Additionally, our highly trained team of archaeologists unearthed a veritable hoard of familial clothing that was preserved in the chariot. The hoard consisted primarily of unmatched socks. In fact, our experts were unable to locate a single matching pair of any clothing item. Based on these findings, it appears that ancient Egyptians lacked the ability to mass-produce clothing and had not yet acquired a taste for fashion or color coordination in general.

Conclusion

Overall findings: While our excavation has pointed to signs of intelligent life, we believe that the average ancient Egyptian family mostly lived out their lives just a notch above uncivilized Neanderthals. We have no idea how such a primitive society could have mustered the ingenuity required to build the pyramids.

Yes, I know that isn't how archaeology works. Historians and archaeologists know how to spot abnormalities and label them as such. It's just fun to think that there was another Wood family way back when who was doing their best to confuse modern historians.

Here's a simple lesson this book has taught me about the past and about history. Someday, some future historian is going to analyze your past. You probably don't want said future historian to categorize you as a relatively boring, relatively adventureless, anthropological normality—a simple cog in the American wheel. You want to be remembered differently. I encourage you to act now to be remembered differently later. Do the things my wife and kids inspire me to do daily. Take risks. Embrace diversity. Travel. Embrace culture. Sing. You want your future historian to look at your past, cry a little, laugh a lot, be moved to take a few adventures, and be encouraged to become a better person, mainly because your future historian is likely to be you.

The Present

Life is what happens to you while you're busy making other plans.[2]

—John Lennon

Today, I walked into the bathroom and found a floor, wall, toilet, shirt, and three-year-old son all saturated in urine. Apparently, when my child finds himself unable to lower his pants fast enough to casually sit down on the toilet, he panics and spins around in circles like some sort of abominable sprinkler. As if that weren't bad enough in and of itself, my three-year-old offender had been attempting to clean up his massive mess by himself with one single, solitary square of toilet paper.

2. John Lennon, "Beautiful Boy," *MetroLyrics*, http://www.metrolyrics.com/beautiful-boy-lyrics-john-lennon.html.

129

In the moment, I wasn't terribly amused by the bathroom situation. I was grossed out to the point of mouth-gagging a bit. Of course, I could say the same for many stories contained in this book.

Regarding the present, my encouragement to you is this. Take time to document the present—the frustrating things, the scary things, and the funny things. If you're anything like me, you'll probably find the situations a lot funnier in the future. You might even decide to write a book someday. Actually, I officially encourage you to write a book someday. If you're a parent, you've got a treasure trove of stories to share. Don't leave it to future historians or future archaeologists to dig them up. Share them. Our messy world could use the laughter you generate as well as the wisdom you've obtained from lessons learned the hard way.

The Future

> We are not fighting for the dead past, but for the living present and the glorious future.[3]
>
> —Frederick Douglass

Our family has so many wonderful memories, so many that it can be easy for me to become overly focused on the past. I sometimes fall into the trap of trying to relive past joys rather than appreciating the present or creating the future. For example, sometimes I miss the days when I could play Nintendo all day while holding a sleeping newborn. Sometimes I miss being able to enjoy a piece of candy without being watched by tiny eyes full of begging and judgment. I miss the days when a guest would ask, "Can I use your restroom?" or "Can I ride in your van?" and I could answer something other than "I don't recommend it."

I could be wrong, but I think there are times when all parents lament their Lysol lives. Even if only for a moment, we daydream about reliving our so-called glory days (although, as anyone who knew me in high school or college will likely attest to, it would be a stretch to claim I ever had so-called glory days about which to daydream). Longing for the past, lamenting the

---

3. "(1864) Frederick Douglass 'The Mission of the War,'" Jan. 28, 2007, *BlackPast*, https://www.blackpast.org/african-american-history/1864-frederick-douglass-mission-war/.

present, and dreading the future—it's a dangerous trap to fall into at any stage in life, especially when you're a parent.

That said, I'm passing along some sage advice that Careese and I received early on in our parenting life. I'm passing it along because I believe that, in a way, this advice became a self-fulfilling parenting prophecy. For us, even with our Struggle Bus life and three teenagers currently residing in our house, each year of parenting has been better than the last, and our parenting life started out pretty great.

We were told that many well-meaning parents overglorify the past to the point that their kids inadvertently do the same. Their kids start to believe that Mom and Dad would rather have some past version of their kid-selves or infant-selves than the current or future version of their kid-selves or teenage-selves or college-selves.

We were told to be wary of using phrases such as "You were so adorable when you were two. What happened?" or "I hope you never become a teenager" or "I hope your sister stays 18-months-old forever" or "You're at the perfect age now. Please don't grow up!"

We were encouraged to do our best to paint the following picture for our children: they started their lives as invaluable to us, but they will become even more valuable to us as they age; we adore them at whatever age they are now, but we'll adore them and appreciate them in new, deeper ways as they grow older and wiser.

We were reminded that becoming a teenager—even in the best of worlds—is a terribly challenging transition. We were told that we parents need to do our best to give our kids reasons to look forward to our relationship with them during their teenage years and not reasons to dread it.

We were told to do everything in our parenting power to instill hope and optimism, to teach our kids that the past was fun and a blessing but that the future can and will be even better.

We were told to remind our kids that their mommy and daddy didn't peak in high school, and neither will they.

We were told that one of the goals of parenting is, from the child's birth, to do your best to use your words and actions to paint a picture of a parent-child relationship that gets better and deeper with age rather than shallower and more distant.

That wisdom has been a God-send for our family, but it isn't how I want to end this book. I'll close with the following bit of wisdom.

We were told by our mentors that we will fail—OFTEN—but we need to fight the urge to let failure keep us down. We were told to "get up, dust yourselves off, learn, and try again."

Boy, were they right! When trying to adhere to that wisdom, I fail often, sometimes in monumentally idiotic ways. In Chapter 6, I mentioned that it's okay to admit you're not okay. Failure is, indeed, a huge part of the human experience—for some of us more than others.

But admitting that you're not okay or failing should never be the end of the road. It should be the beginning of a new, wiser attempt. In fact, I usually learn more when I fail the first time than when I get things right from the beginning. I believe that is the essence of the wisdom we were given: while it is okay to not be okay, it is not okay to stay there. Learn. Pick yourself up, dust yourself off, reattach your fender, learn from the scuff mark you just adorned your van with, hop back into the driver's seat, and start driving again.

If our family's life and our van are any indication of how the world works, some of the best adventures awaiting you in life are disguised as failed plans, shattered dreams, and accidental wrong turns—but only when you keep driving. God does amazing things with our oopsies, uh-ohs, and oh nos. But we have to let him. And that's the thought I leave you with. In the words of Frederick Douglass, we are fighting for "the glorious future."[4] Keep driving through the struggle. All aboard the Struggle Bus!

---

4. "(1864) Frederick Douglass 'The Mission of the War.'"

Acknowledgments

I don't have the time, talent, or treasure to adequately thank the veritable army of humans who have put up with me over the years. But I present to you, dear reader, the following woefully inadequate attempt.

My natural inclination is not adventure. It's safety. It's caution. Had I remained single, I'm confident I would have spent every waking hour holed up in some office, forever working and studying but never serving or living. My people skills would be nonexistent. I'd be an eccentric hoarder of money, information, time, and emotion. Thank God for my wife. When it comes to adventure, she is an icon. She injects excitement into our family. She stretches our comfort zones. She keeps me out of the world of theory and engaged in the much more enjoyable world of trial and failure and success and action. She is my favorite person on this planet. She is my constant motivator. She moms so hard. Without her, there is no Struggle Bus, and I mean that in the best possible way. There is no one I'd rather share this crazy adventure with, this crazy adventure we call life. It takes the best of humanity to put up with me, and she does it daily. And when I said, "Honey, I think I'm going to write a book based on the Craigslist post," she did not say, "That sounds stupid" like most humans would have. She said the words she always says to me about my crazy ideas: "Go for it! I'll be praying about it." She read rough drafts, edited stories, handled my overly fragile ego, and helped me see this thing through to completion. So thank you to my wife, Careese. I love you.

I love my kids. They are fun and creative, and they have a shockingly high tolerance for my daily onslaught of dad jokes. Their faith and grace and hugs are a few of the primary reasons I have stories to write or the joy to write them. Luke, Nathan, Levi, Isaiah, Matthew, Kaylie, Addison, Faith, and Mary—I love you.

A special shout-out to my parents, Steve and Connie Wood, and my in-laws, Jack and Darla Carthel. As our family gets older, we are learning more and more how unique our parents are. I doubt there are many grand-parents out there who have the stamina to babysit as many grandkids as we've often filled their homes with. They've given us the ability to take a weekend or two away every year. They are unwaveringly generous with their grandkids in every way. They are a blessing to us and put up with our crazy ideas, our adventures, our mistakes, and our shenanigans year after year. I love them. I would like to give my parents a special note of thanks for not killing me during my teenage years. Even though they would've been justified in doing so, they restrained themselves. Here's to you, survivors of teenager Josh Wood. Enjoy your grandkids. You've earned them.

I want to be careful not to overstate this. Gail Littlefield is the greatest administrative assistant in the history of the world. Without her ability to diligently maintain my schedule for the last decade or so, this book and many of the adventures contained in it would not have happened. And thanks to the rest of my awesome staff. I couldn't have finished this book without Debbie Ford's constant, smiling presence in the office or her total willingness to tackle any and every random task thrown her way. Aimee Boyett graciously spent hours reading and rereading chapter after revised chapter of this book. Her suggestions improved every one of them. Without her, this book would be extremely less coherent, less organized, and less comprehensible.

Special thanks to my friends Robert Bauman, Mike Isley, and Larry Latham for being a consistent source of prayer and encouragement in my life.

To Sean and Mettie Taylor, David and Mandi Garcia, Matthew Payne, and all of you who have been part of or have visited the church that meets in our home, thank you for taking time out of your Sunday morning to join our island of misfits. You have been an unspeakable blessing to our family.

Thanks to Steve McLean for his editing help as this book came to life. I'm a fan of bending the rules of proper English and forgetting commas and misusing semicolons and misspelling things and using "effect" when I should use "affect" and run-on sentences. Editing this book was, needless to say, no small task.

Finally and most importantly, thanks to Jesus. The ultimate source of my peace, strength, joy, laughter, and hope is found in Christ alone, by grace alone, through faith alone. That is really good news for me because I mess up a lot. If my peace or strength or joy or hope relied on my own success, actions, ability, or good works, I'd be in huge trouble. As it is, though, I have peace, strength, joy, laughter, and hope in the midst of the struggle. Jesus and I both hope you also find those things in the midst of your struggles. All aboard the Struggle Bus!

About the Author

Josh Wood is a native of Amarillo, Texas. He and his wife, Careese, are graduates of Texas A&M University (Gig 'em). Josh went on to obtain his MBA from Baylor University (Sic 'em). Newly wedded Josh and Careese made a number of definitive statements regarding their future, including the following classics:

"We'll never move back to Amarillo."
"We'll have three or four kids. Those kids will never throw fits in Walmart."
"We'll never homeschool our children."
"Home churches are weird."

They live in Amarillo. They have nine kids. They homeschool. They are part of a home church. They've wiped numerous tears off the Walmart floor. Their hobbies include raising children and trying to avoid definitive statements about their future.

CPSIA information can be obtained
at www.ICGtesting.com
Printed in the USA
FSHW021458130420
69127FS

"Wonderful! Absolutely wonderful!"
—Josh's mom

"Dazzling. Magnificent. Marvelous. Remarkable. Thrilling. Wondrous."
—Thesaurus.com synonyms for the word spectacular

"All publishers are welcome to send material for review consideration, but please be aware that we review only a very small percentage of the books we receive, and the odds against a given book receiving a review are long indeed."
—New York Times

"I'm really excited to read an entire book based on a Craigslist post!"
—No one, ever

"I'm so proud of you and our van making us ghetto-famous. I really liked [looks at clock]...Oh no! It's already 6:00 p.m.! Can you please go pick up Kaylie from ballet?"
—Careese Wood, Josh's wife

Struggle Bus: The Van. The Myth. The Legend. is designed to take you, dear reader, on a ride with the Wood family in the van that became an Internet sensation.

This one-of-a-kind literary adventure you are about to embark on is about more than a viral van. It's about managing the wonderful chaos of a family of 11. It's about parenting. It's about marriage. It's about success. It's about failure. It's about faith. It's about fun. It's about a van becoming a metaphor for life as it is given a fun-filled beatdown for the ages.

As you roll along with the Wood family, you just might feel driven to:
- connect a little more with the God who made you.
- give yourself a little more grace when you fail.
- smile and laugh a little more—both at the Wood family's expense and your own.

Hop in, buckle up, hold your nose, laugh, and join the Wood family to explore one of life's fundamental truths: the struggle is real.

ISBN 978-1-63296-392-5

90000

9 781632 963925

LUCIDBOOKS

LinkedIn Made Simple.

FAT
Strategies
in a Thin
Book

RYAN RHOTEN | ANDY FOOTE